TASSAJARA
DINNERS & DESSERTS

In your very own kitchen there is a refuge—
to work as a cook—
like an artist, like a priest.
Sacred space is but one breath away.
Offer yourself up to it.

WITHDRAWN

TASSAJARA
DINNERS & DESSERTS

Dale and Melissa Kent

Photographs by Patrick Tregenza

GIBBS SMITH
TO ENRICH AND INSPIRE HUMANKIND
Salt Lake City | Charleston | Santa Fe | Santa Barbara

We dedicate this book to our teachers and ancestors,
and to all cooks of the past, present, and future.

First Edition
13 12 11 10 09   5 4 3 2 1

Text © 2009 Dale and Melissa Kent
Photographs © 2009 Patrick Tregenza
The excerpts on pages 56 and 210 are from the article "Winter Stew" and are reprinted from *Turning Wheel: The Journal of Socially Engaged Buddhism,* by permission of the Buddhist Peace Fellowship (www.bpf.org).

Published by
Gibbs Smith
P.O. Box 667
Layton, Utah 84041

Orders: 1.800.835.4993
www.gibbs-smith.com

Designed by Black Eye Design
Printed and bound in China
Gibbs Smith books are printed on either recycled, 100% post-consumer waste or
FSC-certified papers.

Library of Congress Cataloging-in-Publication Data

Kent, Dale (Dale B.)
  Tassajara Dinners & Desserts / Dale and Melissa Kent ; photographs by Patrick Tregenza. — 1st ed.
     p. cm.
    ISBN-13: 978-1-4236-0520-1
    ISBN-10: 1-4236-0520-9
    1. Vegetarian cookery. 2. Cookery—Religious aspects—Zen Buddhism. 3. Tassajara Zen
Mountain Center. I. Kent, Melissa. II. Tassajara Zen Mountain Center. III. Title.
    TX837.K4685 2009
    641.5'636—dc22
                              2008034361

We did not invent these recipes.
They are given freely in the heart of the Ventana Wilderness.

Having benefited from these teachings, we offer them to you.

May your time in your kitchen bring you joy.
May the food you cook give nourishment to all.

May all beings be happy, peaceful, and live in freedom.

Wake u
Life is trans
swiftly pas
Beaware
the great ma
Dont waste
Time

contents

acknowledgments

This book has truly been a collaborative effort. The food at Tassajara is a work in progress. Each cook who steps through the door of the kitchen becomes part of the recipe. We offer deep bows to all the cooks and dishwashers who have given their labor and love to the mandala of the Tassajara kitchen.

With a special thanks to all the cooks who contributed recipes and stories, we would like to acknowledge Edward Brown, Annie Somerville, Deborah Madison, Denis Bozulich, Eric Gower, Eva Tuschman, Mary Mocine, Sonja Gardenschwartz, Mark Rutschman-Byler, Charlie Pokorny, Jesse Weins, Mako Voekel, Ramana Lewis, Cristina Cruz, Jeremy Stetter, Gloria Lee, Catherine Gammon, Kathy Egan, Gabe Fields, Ryn Longmaid, Everett Wilson, and Steph Wenderski.

May the recipes and stories they've shared inspire and encourage you to spend time in your kitchen—nourishing yourself and those you love, cooking and being cooked for, for the benefit of all beings.

And finally a thousand bows and our deepest love and gratitude to Jan and Michael, Skip and Paula, Mayumi, Gaelyn, Maya, Kit, Annika and Shaya, Wendy, Robert and Samantha, Keith and Leslie, Cody and Marty, Laura, Rita, Lauren, Heather, JoAnne, Vicci, Terri, Dionne, Christy, Kathy, Amber, Michael W., Tanya, Patrick, Dianne, Melissa and the Gibbs Smith team, and everyone at the Center for Whole Communities.

through the dharma gate

To be asked to be *tenzo* (head of the kitchen) or a guest cook at Tassajara, or even to be assigned to work on the crew in the kitchen for a few days or months, is an invitation to step through a gate—a dharma gate. In a vow that is chanted regularly in Zen temples and practice centers, we say, "Dharma gates are boundless, I vow to enter them;" and though this means that the immeasurable untold moments of our life are not different from a doorway of truth, sometimes we need an extra push to really see that. I would say that being in the kitchen and learning about the truth of our life through cooking and sharing food works for almost everyone.

In the summer of 1968 when I first visited the San Francisco Zen Center, it was still located in Japantown on Bush Street. Suzuki Roshi lived in an apartment in Sokoji Temple, and the students lived mainly in shared Victorian houses in and around the neighborhood. I visited for about a week as a guest student in one of the flats shared by practitioners who had already been to Tassajara Monastery for the ninety-day intensive practice period. One day I was walking by the kitchen and saw two people standing at the kitchen table, chopping onions. Chop, chop, chop. Slice, slice, slice. The sound of the knives cutting through the crisp onions and landing against the wooden board drew me into the doorway, onto the threshold of the kitchen. I watched quietly as they worked along. I was mesmerized. I was riveted. "What are they doing?" I remember asking myself, and immediately there was an answer. "They're chopping onions. They are simply chopping onions." Of course I had seen onions being chopped before.

Throughout my life, my mother had cooked, as had my grandma and aunts (I only saw women in the kitchen around my house). They were good cooks, and I was used to seeing people preparing a meal. But what was it that these people, these Zen students, were doing that seemed so different? Then I realized what it was. They were just chopping onions. That was all. They were relaxed, and quiet, and concentrated, and absorbed in exactly what they were doing—chopping onions! At that moment I realized that there was a way to live that was basic and straightforward and true. The secret, which was never hidden in the first place, was revealed: if you just did whatever you were doing with wholeheartedness, then the practice and joy of one's life was there. I decided, or shall I say vowed, right then, on the threshold of the kitchen, to devote my life to practice. Somehow I intuited that the simplest things included what was most profound in this life. I stepped through the dharma gate and never looked back. About four years later, I was invited to work on the first

kitchen crew at Green Gulch Farm under the direction of Issan Dorsey and later served on several crews at Tassajara until I was appointed head cook.

In the kitchen, whether it is a Zen temple kitchen or not, we can live out the teaching of "Here is the place, here the way unfolds." Here now, in your hands, is the next generation of Tassajara cooking. This is the latest offering of recipes and lore from the hearts of those who stepped through that dharma gate into a world of intimacy with themselves and whoever prepares, shares, and cleans up the meals. Who shares in this activity is, in truth, all beings. The stories and recipes here are meant to support you personally on your path. You are invited and encouraged to cook up a storm and express your love and respect, your awe and gratitude, through the simple act of just cooking.

—Linda Ruth Cutts

introduction

Life at Tassajara is very simple.

You wake up early. You sit quietly, paying attention to your mind and body, learning to let go of everything. You chant. You bow. You eat, and then you wash your bowls. Every minute of your day is filled with support to bring mindfulness, generosity, and kindness to all aspects of your experience.

KITCHEN WORK AS SACRED ACTIVITY

At Tassajara you work in silence and concentrate on what you're doing as if it is the most important thing in the world. You try to feel the earth beneath your feet and the sky above your head. You give the mundane activity of washing vegetables or cooking rice the same care and attention that a priest uses when offering incense in the zendo. You cook and clean as if your grandmother or the Buddha were coming to dinner.

By always putting dishes away in the same place, by moving carefully, and by speaking kindly, you begin to see that harmony exists in all things and to realize the sacred nature of the food you eat.

When you start cooking with a sense of the sacred in mind, you begin to see how your life is entwined with all that exists, and gratitude for everything wells up in your heart.

When you *cook* like this, every stew is special and every grain of rice a miracle. When you begin to *eat* food cooked in this way, you are transformed. You may begin to notice all the ways in which the world is conspiring to support you. You will definitely be healthier and more in tune with yourself. You will find yourself cooking calmly and joyfully. You may even find yourself sitting down on a cushion after the last dish is washed and enjoying your breath as much as the nourishing food in your belly.

WHAT IS A ZEN KITCHEN?

A monastic kitchen differs from a normal restaurant kitchen in that the activity of preparing the food is understood to be spiritual practice. Students working in the Tassajara kitchen have the opportunity to make an effort to be generous, mindful, loving, kind, compassionate, and calm as they prepare food. It is not easy, but with a little effort it is possible to experience true peace in the face of tremendous pressure.

There is something very mysterious that happens when attentive minds prepare and cook food. The food tastes better and simple dishes take on a special elegance.

KITCHEN AS REFUGE

In the zendo there is a particular way to enter, a way to take your seat, a way to greet your neighbor. You know exactly what is expected of you. The room is quiet and calm; the space itself is simple and relaxing, allowing you to feel spacious and free. In the zendo, you sit, chant, and bow. In the winter at Tassajara, it is where you eat most of your meals and spend most of your time. It is an intense and alive container for self-awakening.

The Tassajara kitchen offers this same support. You do not have to worry about small talk or being asked about anything that is not work related. This gives you a certain freedom to be more truly yourself. You are allowed to experience your own mind and body completely.

Being attentive and aware is contagious. If you bring mindfulness to whatever you are doing, it will affect those around you. It is simple but not easy. Mindfulness is a habit that requires sustained effort to cultivate. Monkey mind—the mind that jumps from thought to thought the way a monkey jumps from limb to limb—is always looking for a chance to leap beyond the present moment.

It is easy to be distracted while cutting potatoes. Try to feel your breath sinking deeply into the base of your belly while you chop, and monkey mind may be able to relax and quietly observe. This is zen practice.

EIHEI DOGEN

In the thirteenth century, the founder of Soto Zen, Eihei Dogen, wrote a manual for his disciples about everyday religious life called the *Eihei Shingi*. The first section of that work is called the *Tenzo Kyokun,* or Instructions to the Cook.

The tenzo is the head cook in a Japanese (or Japanese-style) monastery. For Dogen, preparation of food was so important that the head cook at the monastery was a position to be bestowed upon only the most sincere and senior monks who would be able to "function within the way of life of a Buddha" in the context of everyday activity. He tells some inspiring stories of previous tenzos he has known, and the underlying theme to all of them is how extraordinary the most mundane actions can become.

For Dogen, an old man drying mushrooms in the sun or a tenzo walking fourteen miles to get special ingredients for a celebration meal are both shining examples of enlightened activity.

BEING TENZO AT TASSAJARA

When you are given the responsibility of tenzo at Tassajara, it is a great honor—a sign that the elders think you are ready not only to be the administrative head of the kitchen in charge of ordering supplies and training the cooks but also to be the spiritual head of practice in the kitchen. It is not an easy role. Being the tenzo consumes your life and gives you a chance to offer yourself completely—to live for the benefit of all beings.

Dogen said, "My sincerest desire is that you exhaust all the strength and effort of all your lives—past, present, and future, and of every moment of every day—into your practice through the work of the tenzo." In whatever it is that we are doing, there is the chance to lose our small selves. All of

Becoming a Guest Cook

—EVA TUSCHMAN

When I was originally asked to assume the position of guest cook, I felt terrified at the task, yet part of me knew this was a sign to embrace the request. The next day, still wobbling over my decision, I came across a passage from one of Suzuki Roshi's lectures from 1969 in which he says, "Buddha nature is when you say, 'Yes!' or when you become you yourself, or when you forget all about yourself." He goes on to say that our practice is just to say "Yes!" in each moment and jump off from there, not clinging to some idea of old self. It was after reading this that I left the library to find the tenzo and, still full of nervousness, proclaimed, "Yes!"

As the summer progressed, the "I" that was initially fearful of living up to the expected responsibilities began to dissolve. From the first moment of entering the kitchen at the beginning of a shift, there was so much to attend to that the pure activity of continuously moving through the space—carrying produce from the walk-in, delivering trays in and out of the ovens, or hauling gallons of water to a pot—developed into a very intricate choreography. The process of cooking became like a dance, relying over time on a deeply kinesthetic way of knowing and responding to the ingredients and environment. The "I" that in the past was always creating so many hypothetical problems and conceptual boundaries for myself dropped off, and only the direct activity at hand remained.

In this kitchen dance, I learned that the more I could openly face the myriad hindrances that inevitably arose each day and say "Yes!" to them rather than seize up—"What do you mean, there is no more olive oil in the valley!?"—the more fluid and creative the dance evolved. The practice of being guest cook became for me the practice of repeatedly over and over again, in the midst of often uncontrollable circumstances, returning to zazen mind and responding to a situation from a place of constancy, openness, and flexibility. It was a practice of returning to emptiness and seeing this emptiness in all of the seemingly solid forms (and potential problems) of the kitchen. And as Ed Brown and Leslie James reminded me in their own teachings, there was no perfect experience existing somewhere else outside of me that I needed to embody, only the experience that was actually happening.

our self-centered concerns can drop away in a moment spent concentrating on slicing a carrot.

BEING A GUEST COOK

Every spring the tenzo and senior staff invite four students to cook for the summer guest season. When you are invited to be a guest cook, your simple life as a monk changes. There is a large crew to help with prep and dishes, but as a guest cook you are now responsible for planning and preparing elegant five-course meals for eighty guests. Any calm and peaceful energy that you may have cultivated during the fall and winter practice periods is about to be put to the test. There is a pretty good chance that you don't have any professional kitchen experience; and yet, there you are, doing your best, scrambling to get delicious meals out on time.

SPECIAL INGREDIENTS

Many of the recipes in this book were inspired by international cuisines. Some of the ingredients may be unfamiliar to you. Part of the adventure of cooking is gathering the best and most interesting ingredients you can find.

If there are any international markets in your town, start exploring. If you live in a rural area or small town, you might have more of a challenge. Check your local supermarket, and of course you can investigate online for places to buy some of the unfamiliar ingredients like dried cloud ear fungus and ancho chiles.

CHOOSING TO BUY ORGANIC

The most basic element of good food is good ingredients. Organically grown food not only tastes better but is proven to be more nutritious. Buy organic food in whatever amounts you can afford. The value of your health and the health of the earth is beyond measure. Being able to eat food free of toxic herbicides, fungicides, and insecticides is truly a blessing.

During this time of change, as our food system transitions from the "conventional" experiment of petrochemical agriculture back to more sensible and sustainable methods of organic agriculture, it is important to support the farmers who are working hard to bring you healthy chemical-free food. Organic food may be more expensive now, but hopefully someday all food will be organically grown and safe to eat.

EATING LOCALLY

A food shed, like a watershed, is a way to define the region where you live. When you make an effort to eat food grown within a 100- to 200-mile radius from your home, you are walking on the same path that your ancestors walked. Eating food grown in your area and supporting local farmers are ancient acts of wisdom. Farmers markets, Community Supported Agriculture (CSA) programs, Food Baskets, school gardens, and local food cooperatives are all ways to engage in your local food shed.

EATING WHAT IS IN SEASON

Eating what is in season is a sensible choice. Food tastes better and is more delicious when it is local and in season. Eating fruits and vegetables out of season means lots of food miles and a fundamental disconnect between your body and your environment.

The following lists are merely guides—each region is different. As you begin to pay attention to what is available each season, you will notice that what looks good, tastes good, and is a good deal is often in season. Don't even think about it. Just do it!

Fall: apples, artichokes, beets, squash, cauliflower, sweet potatoes, yams, chard, pears, persimmons, pomegranates, plums, cranberries, table grapes, broccoli, carrots, celery, celery root, greens, mushrooms, onions, parsnips, radishes, rutabagas, and turnips;

Winter: turnips, Brussels sprouts, broccoli, mustard greens, collards, kale, celery root, cabbage, radicchio, endive, avocados, grapefruit, persimmons, oranges, lemons, dates, carrots, parsnips, potatoes, rutabaga, romaine lettuce, spinach, winter squash, and beets;

Spring: asparagus, artichokes, fennel, overwintered leeks, peas, shallots, fava beans, baby potatoes, beets, beet greens, dandelion greens, scallions, radishes, spinach, carrots, rhubarb, apricots, strawberries, cherries, arugula, and bok choy;

Summer: apricots, blackberries, blueberries, zucchini, eggplant, corn, tomatoes, okra, chile peppers, bell peppers, onions, figs, nectarines, peaches, melons, cucumbers, lettuces, cilantro, parsley, tarragon, bok choy, green beans, grapes, chard, kale, potatoes, carrots, plums, basil, and tomatillos.

ADVICE TO COOKS AND NON-COOKS

Learn to love prep work. Learn to love holding raw ingredients in your hands and throwing fresh vegetables into pans. Watch in amazement as your fingers learn to hold an onion or a big bunch of greens.

Give yourself permission to spend time just getting the ingredients ready before you even turn on a burner. Getting your workspace in order is the first step. Don't worry if it takes a bit longer. Just try to concentrate on each movement. This is what cooks do. They do this over and over again every day until they no longer have to think about it. At that point, like all artists, they have the capacity to lose themselves in a deeper flow. You can find this space for yourself with practice.

If you think of yourself as someone who is not a cook, we invite you to join the party. Esoteric truths and answers to many mysteries can be uncovered in a bubbly sink of soapy water and dirty dishes. Dive in and enjoy!

starters

Antipasto Plate 20

Ginger Hummus 22

Baba Ghanoush 23

Yogurt-Whipped Feta with Radishes 23

Guacamole 24

Salsa Fresca 24

Baked Hummus with Yogurt and Lemon 26

Gyoza 27

Wontons 28

Sushi 31

Sweet Sesame Hijiki 32

Pickled Ginger 33

Spring Rolls with Dipping Sauces 34

Grandma Chu's Sweet and Sour Marinated Asparagus 37

Antipasto Plate

Beets, mushrooms, olives, and some grilled zucchini and peppers make for a colorful and substantial platter that can be set up well ahead for dinner or thrown together for an elegant lunch.

1 bunch Chioggia beets
Mushrooms
Salt and pepper
Olive oil
Minced garlic
Fresh herbs

Olives
Fresh lemon zest and juice
Feta cheese
Zucchini
Bell peppers, red and yellow

Scrub the beets and cook them unpeeled in a pressure cooker for 7 to 10 minutes, or roast them in an oven at any convenient temperature above 350 degrees until a knife easily pierces the largest beet. (Boiling or steaming is also a possibility.) Expect large beets to take as long as 40 to 45 minutes to cook, smaller ones about 25 minutes. Sweet young beets need little other than some salt and pepper and a tablespoon or two of olive oil. Also, a little Reduced Balsamic Vinegar (see page 204) can make beets really sparkle.

Toss mushrooms with a little olive oil, salt, and pepper. Roast at 400 degrees for about 25 minutes. They should sizzle and start to brown. Put mushrooms in a bowl and toss with garlic and a few table-spoons chopped parsley or tarragon. Let them sit and marinate while they cool.

Sauté olives with a few sprigs of fresh herbs like thyme or rosemary with a pinch or so of lemon zest. Sauté just to heat through and squeeze some lemon juice over top before serving. Slice or crumble feta into bite-sized pieces and bring up to room temperature before serving.

Split a zucchini in half lengthwise. Score the flesh with a paring knife and baste with olive oil. Cook over hot coals for a few minutes per side until blackened in spots. If you don't want to mess with a fire, line up the zucchini on sheet pans and bake at 425 degrees for about 20 to 30 minutes, or until thoroughly cooked through.

Grill bell peppers over hot coals until the skin is blistered. Put them in a paper bag to steam for 10 to 15 minutes and then peel them. Do not rinse in water. Remove and discard the stems and seeds, and then slice the pepper into thin strips or bite-size pieces.

SERVES 6

Ginger Hummus

None of the hummus you buy at the store will be as satisfying as what you mix up on your own. Even if you're using a can of cooked chickpeas, homemade hummus is far superior to store-bought varieties. A can of beans is a more sustainable choice than a plastic package that has to rely on refrigeration to stay fresh.

2 cups chickpeas, checked for rocks, washed in several rinses of water, and soaked overnight (if not using a pressure cooker)

2 inches ginger, peeled and cut into coins or grated

4 garlic cloves, peeled

1 teaspoon cumin seeds, toasted and ground

1 teaspoon coriander seeds, toasted and ground

2 to 3 tablespoons olive oil

¼ to ½ cup tahini

Juice of 2 lemons

Salt

Simmer the chickpeas in a large pot with ginger and enough water to cover by 4 inches for about 2 hours (it may take as many as 3 or as little as 1 hour, depending on their age). They should be perfectly soft and mushy. Drain chickpeas and reserve the cooking liquid. Purée chickpeas with remaining ingredients and about ¼ cup of the cooking liquid. Taste to see if you want the higher quantity of oil or tahini.

SERVES 6–8

A Crisis

—CHARLIE POKORNY

One of my clearest memories of being tenzo in the summer was when I made a mistake—I forgot to get beets for a guest cook. I felt awful having to tell him that I had forgotten to order his beets—that there were no beets for his chilled borscht soup the next day. I felt the tension of a crisis coming on.

When I told the cook, though, he just shrugged and said, "That's okay. How about black bean chili?"

"Sure! No problem."

It was a short crisis.

Baba Ghanoush

Even people who think they don't like eggplant often love to dip warm pita bread into this simple purée of roasted eggplant, garlic, and tahini. Use the most tender, fresh eggplants you can find. When serving this to the guests at Tassajara, we like to garnish it with a little chopped parsley or cilantro.

2 large eggplants (about 2½ pounds)
6 to 8 garlic cloves, minced
½ cup tahini

Juice of 2 or 3 lemons
Salt
Extra virgin olive oil (optional)

Before putting the eggplants in the oven, make some holes with a fork or slashes with a knife on all sides, just enough to let the steam out of the skin as it cooks. Roast the eggplants at 425 degrees for about 30 minutes until the flesh is perfectly soft and the skin is getting loose. Cool for 10 to 20 minutes, or just enough so you can handle it comfortably. Peel the eggplant and purée or mash it together with the garlic and tahini. Add lemon juice and salt to taste. Add a little extra virgin olive oil, if desired.

SERVES 6–8

Yogurt-Whipped Feta with Radishes

Serve this simple appetizer alongside hummus, pita bread, and other Mediterranean salads.

1½ cups Greek yogurt or other thick
   European-style yogurt
½ to ¾ cup crumbled feta cheese
Extra virgin olive oil
½ fresh lemon

¼ cup radishes, thinly sliced into rounds,
   then cut into half moons
Salt and pepper
Fresh parsley or mint leaves

In a food processor, whip the yogurt and cheese to desired consistency. Drizzle in a little olive oil and a squeeze of fresh lemon juice. Stir in the radishes and taste for salt and pepper. (You may not need to add much salt because of the feta cheese.) Garnish with a spoon of olive oil, freshly cracked pepper, and mint or parsley leaves.

SERVES 4–6

Guacamole

Guacamole is traditionally loaded with salsa, onion, and garlic, but this homemade guacamole with lime and cilantro is a special treat!

2 to 3 avocados	½ cup roughly chopped cilantro
1 lime	Salt

The avocados need to be ripe but not those overripe "good for guacamole" ones. Mash the flesh, but not to a pulp—keep some nice chunks in the mixture. Add some lime juice as you mash to keep it looking fresh. Chop the cilantro right before it goes into the guacamole. Add salt to taste and stir together.

NOTE: *All of the proportions are variable according to taste, ingredients, and what you're serving it with. It's nice when the lime, salt, and cilantro are all fairly strong, but not so strong as to overpower the creamy taste of the avocados.*

SERVES 4–6

Salsa Fresca

This salsa is best at the height of summer when the tomatoes and peppers are fresh from the garden.

2 cups roughly chopped tomatoes	1 to 2 limes
1 to 3 jalapeños	½ bunch cilantro, finely chopped
2 garlic cloves	Salt and pepper
¾ cup diced onion	

Put the tomatoes in a bowl. Mince the jalapeños and garlic as small as you can and then toss with the tomatoes. Add the onion, squeeze the lime(s) over the mixture, add the cilantro, and stir. Add salt and pepper to taste.

SERVES 4–6

"The Chemistry of Transformation:
The combination of intention, food, and heat.
The combination of meditation, intention, and practice.
This is the chemistry of transformation for nourishing and benefiting all beings."

—SONJA GARDENSCHWARTZ

Baked Hummus with Yogurt and Lemon

This is a delicious variation on the traditional meze *(appetizer) of hummus. Serve hot from the oven with freshly baked pita bread.*

1¼ cups dried chickpeas or about 3½ cups
    cooked or canned
¼ cup good-quality extra virgin olive oil,
    plus more for drizzling
Juice and zest of 1 lemon
3 small garlic cloves, roughly minced
2 teaspoons cumin seeds
3 to 4 tablespoons tahini

5 tablespoons European-style plain yogurt
Salt and freshly ground pepper
1 teaspoon paprika
Fresh nutmeg (optional)
Lemon slices, toasted pine nuts, or fresh
    mint leaves for garnish

If you are using dried chickpeas, sort and wash them before covering them in plenty of cold water to soak for a minimum of 6 hours or preferably overnight. Drain the chickpeas and bring to a boil in a large pot of cold water. Once the water has boiled, reduce the heat and simmer for 1 hour over low heat, or until the chickpeas are soft. You may need to skim the water of any foam that rises to the surface. When the chickpeas are cooked through, drain. (Skip this step if using precooked chickpeas.)

Preheat the oven to 350 degrees. In a food processor, purée the chickpeas with the olive oil, lemon juice and zest, garlic, and cumin. Slowly add the tahini in a stream and then add the yogurt until the purée is smooth and integrated. Alternatively, you can also mash the ingredients by hand, which will produce a more textured spread. Taste and season with more lemon juice and zest, salt, and freshly ground pepper. For a lighter purée, add more yogurt.

Using a spatula, transfer the mixture to a small ovenproof dish, spreading it lightly on the top. Drizzle with olive oil and sprinkle with paprika for color. You may wish to add some additional shavings of fresh nutmeg. Bake for 15 minutes or until the top is a golden brown. Garnish with thin slices of lemon, toasted pine nuts, or fresh mint leaves.

SERVES 4–6

Gyoza

This recipe calls for a lot of fine chopping. Use a Cuisinart if you don't want to prep all the ingredients by hand.

¾ cup finely minced mushrooms

½ cup thinly sliced scallions

½ serrano pepper, seeded and finely minced

2 tablespoons salt, divided

2 teaspoons finely ground flax seed

1 cup finely minced cabbage

½ cup finely minced carrot

2 to 3 garlic cloves, minced

1½ teaspoons finely minced ginger

6 mint leaves, chiffonade

⅓ cup finely chopped walnuts

1 to 2 teaspoons soy sauce

1 teaspoon pepper

Gyoza skins (see Wontons, page 28)

2 to 3 tablespoons peanut or canola oil

Sauté mushrooms, scallions, and serrano slightly with 1 teaspoon salt; drain and save liquid. Put mixture into a medium bowl. Grind the flax seed into a sticky paste with the mushroom liquid using a mortar and pestle. Add flax to bowl along with all remaining ingredients except the gyoza skins. Mix thoroughly, squeezing mixture together with fingers.

Heap 1 level tablespoon filling towards the front of the gyoza skin round. Fold top half over to make a semicircle and pinch edges together firmly to seal. Bring two points slightly together to make a crescent shape. Continue in this way until all the filling is used up.

Brush a large lidded frying pan with oil and heat over medium-high heat. Fit gyozas snuggly in concentric circles until pan is full. Fry for 4 to 5 minutes , or until they are brown and firm underneath, moving them around slightly so they do not stick. Pour in just enough water to cover the bottom of the pan and cover immediately with a tight-fitting lid. Steam for 5 to 6 minutes, or until all the water has steamed off and the tops of gyozas feel firm and not sticky. Serve immediately.

SERVES 6–8

Wontons

Wonton skins are easy to buy, but you can make fresh pasta for homemade wontons. They are a labor of love and fun to make. Follow the method for making fresh pasta but use the following formula.

4 cups flour
1 teaspoon salt
2 eggs

2 teaspoons peanut oil
1 cup cold water

FILLING

2 tablespoons mushroom or plain soy
   sauce
1 tablespoon Shaoxing wine or dry sherry
½ tablespoon black vinegar or balsamic
   vinegar
1 tablespoon sesame oil
3 scallions, minced

1 teaspoon minced fresh ginger
½ teaspoon minced garlic
1 (8-ounce) can water chestnuts, drained
   and minced (optional)
⅓ teaspoon pepper
1 pound tofu, crumbled
1 egg

Using the flour, salt, eggs, oil, and cold water, follow the directions for Fresh Pasta in the grains chapter on page 148. Cut sheets of pasta into 3-inch squares or rounds and dust with rice flour or cornstarch so they won't stick together. Wrapped, they last for months in the freezer, or 3 days if refrigerated. This recipe makes about 50 wonton skins.

For the filling, mix together all the ingredients except the tofu and egg. Marinate tofu with this mixture. Taste for flavor and then let rest for at least 30 minutes.

When you are ready to make the wontons, stir the egg into the filling mixture to help bind it all together. (You can leave the egg out but the filling will not hold together in the same way.)

Hold a wonton skin in the palm of one hand and put about 1 teaspoon filling into the center of the skin. Wet the edges with a little water and then fold opposing edges together; pinch to seal. Cook wontons in boiling salted water for about 5 minutes; drain. Make sure to simmer them for about 5 minutes to complete their cooking.

You can also deep-fry filled wontons in peanut oil at 365 degrees until they are browned.

SERVES 6–8

Learning to Cook

—DALE KENT

When I first began cooking at Tassajara, I knew very little about food. I had worked as a baker for a few years, so I could eyeball a tablespoon in the palm of my hand and crack a lot of eggs really quickly. I knew a little bit about organization and multitasking, and I understood how to stop when you heard the bell ring on the stove.

My first tenzo, Robert, taught me how to taste food and pay attention to all the little details of a dish. My second tenzo, Charlie, taught me about generosity and the gift of fearlessness. My first guest cook partner, Eleanor, taught me to plan and move quickly. The kitchen crews I worked with taught me to be aware of the space we shared and the fragility of our hearts.

Potatoes taught me to believe in the power of faith and prayer.

Hot cereal taught me patience.

But I never really learned how to cook until I spent the summer watching Jerome make meals for the guests. Watching Jerome cook, I learned about playfulness and art. Jerome had an infectious passion for food. He came to Tassajara after cooking at Chez Panisse for a dozen years. The first summer that I was a guest cook, he humbly worked on the crew, doing dishes and prep work. I didn't pay much attention to him until the day the asparagus arrived a little late for my dinner.

I was nervous about cooking one of my first guest meals when I walked past this guy peeling the bottom half of each asparagus stalk. It seemed like it would be an endless project so, knowing nothing about asparagus, I asked him what he was doing. He said not to worry, it wouldn't take long, and then he picked one up and showed me how he was removing the fibrous bits. He also said they would cook more evenly and look "kinda cool, y' know?" I didn't say a word other than thanks. He was almost done turning eleven pounds of asparagus into a mountain of jade green jewels.

Sushi

Traditionally it takes at least a decade of training to become a sushi chef, but at Tassajara, perfectly acceptable vegetarian sushi is made with little or no training. The rice might be a little mushy or sometimes too sweet or too dry, and the grains might not be as distinctive as they would be if a master had prepared it, but it always tastes good and sushi is fun to make.

1 cup short-grain white rice (sushi rice)*	2 tablespoons rice vinegar
1⅔ cups water	1 tablespoon brown sugar
1 piece kombu (seaweed), about 2 inches	¼ teaspoon salt
2 scallions, trimmed	2 to 4 sheets nori
1 carrot, cut into long, thin strips	½ avocado

Wash the rice in several rinses of cold water and drain well.

In a heavy-bottom 3-quart saucepan, bring the water and kombu to a boil. Add the rice and return to a boil. Reduce heat to medium and boil, covered, for 5 minutes. Reduce heat to low and simmer for 15 to 20 minutes more, or until the water is absorbed. Remove the kombu and let the rice stand for 10 minutes.

While the rice cooks, prepare the scallions and carrot. Blanch for 1 minute in boiling water. Scoop them out and plunge them into a bowl of ice water to preserve their color and just a little crunch.

In a small saucepan over low heat, mix the vinegar, sugar, and salt just until dissolved.

When the rice is ready, put it in a wide bowl and sprinkle a little of the vinegar mixture over the top. Fan the rice as you use a sort of sideways slashing motion with a wooden paddle or spatula to cut in the vinegar. (You are trying to separate the individual grains of rice and coat them each with the sweet vinegar. You also want to release as much steam from the rice as quickly as possible without breaking the rice grains into little pieces.) Continue adding vinegar and stirring while fanning until the rice looks glossy and has cooled to room temperature.

Put the nori shiny side down on a sushi rolling mat if you have one. If you don't have a rolling mat, use 3 to 4 layers aluminum foil folded to the size of a sheet of nori. Spread half the rice evenly onto

recipe continued on next page

one piece of nori, leaving at least a few inches of uncovered nori on the edge farthest from you. Wet hands are the key to keeping the rice from sticking to you instead of itself.

Slice the avocado thinly and put strips down the center of the rice. Gently press the scallions and carrots onto the avocado and roll the sushi into a tight bundle with the vegetables in the center. Take care not to include the mat into your roll. Seal the roll with a little water on the exposed strip of nori. Cut sushi with a thin, wet knife and serve within a few hours.

*Sushi rice needs to cool quickly after it is cooked so that the grains remain separate and whole, and dry out just enough to keep from being too sticky. At Tassajara we put the rice in a large bowl and toss it with sweet vinegar while someone fans the rice with a sheet tray. In Japan, they use specially made wooden bowls that help soak up excess moisture from the rice. A large wooden salad bowl works well if you have one.

SERVES 4–6

Sweet Sesame Hijiki

A lot of people who don't think they like seaweed often like this simple preparation. Serve small piles of this sweet seaweed as a condiment with rice or sushi, or mix it in with sautéed carrots for a beautiful side dish.

1 ounce hijiki, soaked for 10 to 15 minutes (until softened) in warm water*	1 tablespoon soy sauce
2 tablespoons mirin	½ tablespoon rice vinegar
	½ tablespoon toasted sesame oil

Rinse hijiki in several changes of water, as it can be rather dirty and full of sand; drain in a strainer. Dress hijiki with remaining ingredients. Taste to make sure the flavors all balance each other. This tasty seaweed salad keeps in the refrigerator for at least a week or two.

Most hijiki sold in the West is what the Japanese refer to as "dust," small little pieces no longer than a quarter of an inch. Good-quality hijiki is much larger and often needs to be cut or broken into bite-size pieces.

SERVES 4–6

Pickled Ginger

The jars of pickled ginger you find at the grocery store are pretty good, but it is much more economical and fun to make your own. Add half of a small red beet to the pan to give the ginger color. The pickling process will naturally turn the ginger mildly pink after about one week. Adding a little beet gives you color without the wait.

4 to 6 inches ginger, cut into razor thin
    slices or small matchsticks
1 to 2 teaspoons salt

2 cups vinegar
½ cup sugar
½ small beet (optional)

Toss ginger with salt and let sit for 30 minutes.

In a small saucepan, simmer vinegar, sugar, and beet until the sugar is dissolved and the vinegar is beautifully colored by the beet, about 5 minutes. Rinse most of the salt from the slices of ginger and put them in the pan with the pickling juice. Let sit for at least 30 minutes before draining and serving. Store leftovers covered with pickling juice in a sterilized jar for up to a month.

SERVES 4–6

Wasabi

—DALE KENT

The amount of water that you need to reconstitute wasabi powder is surprisingly small. Reconstituted wasabi seems to get stronger and more pungent if you let it sit for 30 minutes or so after mixing it.

I remember one cook mixed together a batch of wasabi early in the afternoon. She covered it with a lid and went about doing everything else she needed to do to prepare for her sushi dinner. When the cook lifted the lid off of it, she coughed and gasped as her eyes started watering from the cloud of wasabi-infused air that came up from the bowl. I was at my desk a few yards away and my eyes started watering too. I couldn't believe how potent that little bowl of wasabi had become.

Spring Rolls with Dipping Sauces

The hardest thing about making spring rolls is taking care not to tear the delicate rice paper wrappers. This just takes patience and practice. The people who eat them will appreciate your diligence!

SPRING ROLLS

1 package dried rice stick noodles (very thin, vermicelli-style noodles)

1 package rice paper wrappers (8 ½-inch rounds)

1½ cups shredded carrots

1½ cups (2½-inch-long) cucumber matchsticks

16 leafy (2½-inch) cilantro sprigs

¾ cup thinly sliced mint ribbons

1 cup thinly sliced scallions

SPRING ROLL DIPPING SAUCE

¼ cup rice vinegar

½ cup soy sauce

2 tablespoons sesame oil

2 tablespoons water

2 tablespoons peeled, minced ginger

PEANUT DIPPING SAUCE

Peanut oil

1 tablespoon minced garlic

1 teaspoon peeled, minced ginger

½ teaspoon crushed red pepper flakes

1 cup water

2 tablespoons soy sauce

Juice from 1 lime

¾ cup chunky peanut butter

1 tablespoon brown sugar

1 tablespoon finely chopped mint

CHILE OIL

1 cup Thai chiles

1 cup peanut oil

To make the spring rolls, soak the rice stick noodles in warm water until soft, about 30 minutes; drain and allow to air-dry slightly.

Use a shallow pan of hot water to soak the first rice paper wrapper until it is pliable. Gently remove it from the water with your fingers and spread it flat on a cutting board. About 1 inch from the bottom of the wrapper, center a small mound of rice stick noodles, about 1½ tablespoons of carrot, a few cucumber matchsticks, a sprig of cilantro, a pinch of mint, and 1 tablespoon of scallions. Gently begin rolling from the bottom, tucking the sides in snugly as you roll. Take care not to overstuff the rolls or they will become difficult to manage. Arrange on a serving tray and serve with dipping sauces within a couple of hours.

To make the spring roll dipping sauce, whisk all ingredients together. Serve in small dipping bowls.

To make the peanut dipping sauce, coat the bottom of a small saucepan with the peanut oil and heat over medium heat. Add garlic, ginger, and red pepper flakes. Stir constantly until lightly browned. Add water, soy sauce, lime juice, peanut butter, and brown sugar. Cook for a few minutes until thickened. Remove from heat and stir in mint. Serve in small dipping bowls.

To make the chile oil, grind Thai chiles in a spice grinder. Mix the ground chiles with peanut oil. Bring to a simmer over medium heat. Remove from heat and allow the mixture to steep overnight before straining it. Serve with spring rolls or as a condiment for vegetable stir-fries. Store in a glass jar in the refrigerator.

SERVES 6–8

Grandma Chu's Sweet and Sour Marinated Asparagus

A quick appetizer for any Asian-themed meal. This recipe is great to throw together before you start preparing a meal so that it can sit and marinate. You can substitute other cool, crunchy veggies as well as alternative sweeteners. The important thing here is to find a balance of sweet, sour, salt, sesame, and spicy (optional) that excites your palate!

2 pounds fresh asparagus (can substitute cucumbers, radishes, etc.)

1 teaspoon salt

2 tablespoons light soy sauce or tamari (not lite or low-sodium)

2 tablespoons rice vinegar, black vinegar, or balsamic vinegar

1 tablespoon sugar

1 teaspoon dark sesame oil (the strong-flavored Asian kind, not the light cooking oil)

1 teaspoon hot chile sauce (optional)

Bend or break off and discard the tough asparagus root ends. Blanch the asparagus in boiling water for 1 minute, then drain and immerse in cold water to stop the cooking. Chop into 1½-inch lengths.

Whisk the remaining ingredients together and pour over the asparagus. Marinate for at least 30 minutes (the longer the better) before serving. Can chill for 10 minutes in the refrigerator before serving.

SERVES 6–8

vegetable side dishes

Arugula Salad with Radishes, Oranges, Feta, and Mint 41

Four Ways to Cook Asparagus 42

Roasted Green Beans with Basil and Hazelnuts 44

Sichuan Green Beans 45

Stir-Fried Broccoli with Garlic 46

Sesame Soy Slaw 47

Coleslaw with Oranges, Cilantro, Cumin, and Lime 47

Broccoli and Red Bell Pepper Salad 49

Cucumber-Tomato Salad 49

Corn-on-the-Cob with Lime Chipotle Butter 50

Pungent Cucumber Salad with Black Sesame and Ginger 52

Mint Cilantro Chutney 54

Raita 54

Tamarind Chutney 55

Daikon Salad with Lime-Ume Dressing 57

Sweet Glazed Daikon 57

Sichuan Eggplant 58

Roasted Fennel and Radicchio 59

Easy Greens with Soy Sauce and Honey 60

Kashmiri-Style Greens with Roasted Potatoes 61

Crispy Baked Kale 62

Ginger Apricot Chutney 62

Stir-Fried Pea Shoots 65

Moroxican Spiced Potatoes 66

Roasted Fingerling Potatoes and Corn in Dijon Vinaigrette 68

Spinach with Sesame 69

Ginger Mashed Yams 70

Roasted Yams with Ancho Chile Paste 70

Roasted Winter Squash 71

Roasted Zucchini with Garlic Oil 71

Arugula Salad with Radishes, Oranges, Feta, and Mint

This Moroccan-inspired salad can be tossed and served in a bowl or made as a composed salad arranged on a platter and drizzled with the vinaigrette. In the latter form, the salad presents a more traditional meze, or appetizer. For different combinations, consider including wedges of hard-boiled egg, oil-cured black olives, or thin shavings of fennel.

1/3 cup pistachios
3 blood oranges (or navel oranges, if blood are unavailable)
1 bunch radishes

1 pound arugula leaves
4 ounces feta cheese
Handful of fresh mint sprigs
North African Vinaigrette (see page 203)

Toast the pistachios at 350 degrees for 12 to 15 minutes, or until they release their oils and fragrance.

Contouring the orange, carve away the skin and white pith of the fruit. Using a serrated knife, slice the orange into thin transparent pinwheel rounds.

Wash the radishes and leave them whole or cut them into wedges or slices. Arrange the washed arugula on a large platter. Layer the oranges with slices of feta cheese. You may prefer to crumble the feta or leave it in a block and allow your guests to cut it apart themselves. Compose the plate with the radishes, then sprinkle with the pistachios and a handful of torn mint leaves. Re-whisk the vinaigrette and drizzle over the platter with a spoon. Dust with coarse sea salt and freshly cracked pepper.

SERVES 4

Four Ways to Cook Asparagus (or any vegetable)

Peel the bottom half of each asparagus stalk to remove most of the fibrous bits. This helps the asparagus cook more evenly and makes them look like beautiful jade green jewels.

ROASTED

2 pounds asparagus
Olive oil
Salt

Preheat oven to 450 degrees. Soak asparagus spears in water to wash them. Swish them around a bit to make sure that all the sand and dirt gets rinsed from the tips. Snap off an inch or two from the woody bottom of each spear.

Put the asparagus on a lightly oiled sheet pan and drizzle a few tablespoons olive oil over top. Roll them around with your hands to thoroughly coat with oil. Roast for about 15 minutes, or until softened and starting to brown. Shake the pan a few times while they cook to turn them so they color on more than one side. Sprinkle salt over top and serve warm or cold.

SAUTÉED

2 tablespoons olive oil
1 teaspoon minced garlic
2 pounds asparagus, trimmed and sliced
diagonally into $1/4$-inch pieces

Salt and freshly ground black pepper
1 small lemon

Heat olive oil in a skillet over high heat. Add the garlic and sauté for 15 to 20 seconds. Toss in the asparagus and some salt, and continue to sauté over high heat until the asparagus is tender and cooked through. Season with pepper, taste for salt, and squeeze lemon juice over top just before serving.

    2 pounds asparagus, trimmed
    Water
    Salt and freshly ground black pepper

Place whole asparagus spears in a skillet and cover with cold water. Bring to a boil and simmer for about 10 minutes until the fattest spear can easily be pierced. Lift asparagus out of the pan with a pair of tongs or drain in a colander. Season with salt and pepper, and serve warm; or plunge the asparagus into a bowl of ice water to stop the cooking and drain on kitchen towels until you need it.

BOILED WITH BUTTER SAUCE

2 pounds asparagus, trimmed and sliced into 1-inch lengths
$^1/_3$ to $^1/_2$ cup water

$^1/_2$ teaspoon salt
4 tablespoons butter, cut into small pieces
$^1/_4$ cup finely chopped parsley

Put the asparagus, water, and salt in a skillet; cover and bring to a boil. Boil $1^1/_2$ minutes and then add the butter and parsley. Shake the pan vigorously over high heat and boil for about 30 seconds, or until the sauce thickens and foams. As soon as it foams, remove from the heat and serve.

SERVES 4–6

Roasted Green Beans with Basil and Hazelnuts

These are certainly not the most beautiful green beans, but they are always a crowd-pleaser. Oven roasting green beans concentrates their flavor and makes them absolutely delicious.

1 pound green beans	2 to 3 garlic cloves, minced
2 to 3 tablespoons olive oil	$^1/_4$ cup chopped basil leaves
Salt and pepper	$^1/_3$ cup hazelnuts, toasted and skinned

Toss the green beans with olive oil, salt, pepper, and garlic. Bake in a single layer on sheet pans at 500 degrees for 15 to 20 minutes. Shake them once or twice during cooking so that they color evenly. They should be soft and tender and flecked with brown spots when done. Add basil to the beans while they are still warm. Sprinkle with roughly chopped hazelnuts and serve hot or cold.

SERVES 4–6

How to Cook Vegetables and to Let Go of Trying to Please Everybody

—CHARLIE POKORNY

I think with so few other things to focus on, food becomes disordinately important, especially during the winter. It was difficult being tenzo when there was disfavor with the food.

With cooking green vegetables, I finally gave up trying to please people, because there were some who wanted them overcooked to be easier to digest, others wanted them undercooked to retain more nutritional value, and some wanted it done just right because . . . why not?

I ended up feeling that however they were cooked was just fine. I found I liked keeping it mixed up to keep somebody happy at least some of the time and, of course, to let go of making everybody happy all the time.

Sichuan Green Beans

These green beans are pretty authentic tasting even though a Chinese cook would not blanch a vegetable before putting it in a stir-fry. Most traditional Chinese cooks make sure their vegetables are perfectly dry before putting them in the wok. Of course, they cook over much higher heat than we do so the beans cook in just a few minutes. If you do not own a wok, a cast-iron skillet works well to stir-fry the green beans.

2 tablespoons tamari
1 tablespoon dry sherry
1 teaspoon sugar (or honey)
½ teaspoon cornstarch
¼ teaspoon white pepper
¼ teaspoon red pepper
¼ teaspoon dry mustard
2 tablespoons water

1½ pounds green beans
2 tablespoons peanut oil
1 tablespoon minced garlic
1 tablespoon minced ginger
3 scallions, thinly sliced
1 to 2 tablespoons sesame oil
Salt

Combine tamari, sherry, sugar, cornstarch, peppers, mustard, and water, and mix until sugar is dissolved; set aside.

Blanch green beans briefly so that they are still crisp but not raw.

Heat peanut oil in a wok until it just begins to smoke and then toss in drained green beans. Fry until crisp-tender and skins are shriveled and blackened in spots. Add garlic and ginger, and fry until cooked through, about a minute or so. Be very careful not to let the garlic and ginger burn.

Add sauce towards the end of cooking and toss with the scallions, sesame oil, and salt just before serving.

SERVES 4–6

Stir-Fried Broccoli with Garlic

If cooking a lot of broccoli, steam it for a couple of minutes before putting it in the pan. This allows the thicker, crunchier parts of the florets to get a head start on cooking and makes the stir-frying go along more quickly. Stir-fry in a big cast-iron skillet rather than a wok.

2 to 3 tablespoons oil*
3 to 4 garlic cloves, crushed with the side
  of a knife but kept whole

1 bunch broccoli
Salt and pepper

Heat a pan over high heat and add oil. (Use more than you might think. The oil is infused with the garlic flavor and then becomes a sort of dressing for the broccoli, so it needs to coat each piece.)

As soon as the oil starts to heat up to the right temperature, it will begin to shimmer. Add the garlic and let sizzle in the oil for a few seconds. Remove the garlic and reserve; add the broccoli. Keep the broccoli moving in the pan. It should take about 5 to 7 minutes to be well done with a few nicely browned spots. Mince the garlic and toss it into the pan at the last second. Add salt and pepper to taste and serve immediately.

When stir-frying, it is important to use good high-quality oil with a high-heat tolerance so that it does not start smoking at the high heat that you need to cook an authentic stir-fry. Canola, coconut, peanut, safflower, or sesame oils are all fine to use. Olive oil starts smoking and breaking down at low temperatures, which makes it taste bad and is also bad for you.

SERVES 4–6

Sesame Soy Slaw

This recipe works well with Napa cabbage, but the colorful contrast between the red cabbage and scallions looks beautiful together.

1 teaspoon minced ginger
1/2 small red onion, minced
2 tablespoons rice wine vinegar
1/8 teaspoon chili powder or sauce
   (optional)
1 teaspoon soy sauce

1 teaspoon light brown sugar
4 tablespoons sesame oil
1 small red cabbage, shredded
6 scallions, shredded
4 tablespoons toasted and chopped
   peanuts

In a bowl, combine the ginger and onion with the vinegar and let stand for 10 to 15 minutes. Stir in the chili powder, soy sauce, and sugar. Whisk in the sesame oil and toss together with the cabbage, scallions, and peanuts. Let sit and marinate for at least 10 minutes before serving.

SERVES 4–6

Coleslaw with Oranges, Cilantro, Cumin, and Lime

This Mexican-inspired slaw is good with red or green cabbage. A little of both is always pretty. Add slivers of jalapeño or serrano peppers if you want a little heat.

1 small cabbage, shredded
1 medium orange, peeled and sectioned or
   cut into bite-size pieces

Cumin Lime Vinaigrette (see page 201)
Salt
3 tablespoons chopped cilantro

Toss cabbage and orange pieces with dressing. Taste for salt and serve immediately, or refrigerate and let sit for up to a few hours. Toss the cilantro in just before serving.

SERVES 4–6

Broccoli and Red Bell Pepper Salad

Broccoli and Red Bell Pepper Salad

This simple salad is a colorful addition to any meal. Serve it with a hearty soup for lunch in the fall or as part of a light dinner in the heat of the summer.

Honey Dijon Vinaigrette (see page 202)
2 heads broccoli, broken into small florets
    and blanched for 3 minutes

2 red bell peppers, cut into 2-inch strips

Make the vinaigrette according to directions. Pour vinaigrette over the broccoli and peppers, and toss. Marinate for at least 2 hours before serving. Serve chilled.

SERVES 6–8

Cucumber-Tomato Salad

It's best to prepare this salad just before serving.

1 clove garlic
1 serrano chile, seeded
1 cucumber, diced*
2 tablespoons lemon juice

3 tablespoons light soy sauce
1 teaspoon sugar
1 tomato, diced or cut into wedges
1 tablespoon roasted and chopped peanuts

Mince the garlic and chile, and add to the cucumber. Add the lemon juice, soy sauce, sugar, and tomato to the cucumber mixture and stir. Add peanuts just before serving; turn once and serve.

For English or hot-house cucumber, just wash and dry, then dice or cut into matchsticks. For regular cucumber, peel and seed, then dice or cut into matchsticks.

SERVES 4

Corn-on-the-Cob with Lime Chipotle Butter

Flavored butters are always a hit, and the dark smokiness of the chipotles paired with simply cooked fresh corn makes you think the corn was grilled, rather than boiled. Make more of the flavored butter so you have extra; wrapped well, it will last for a year in the freezer and a few weeks in the fridge.

LIME CHIPOTLE BUTTER

1 stick butter, softened

2 to 3 teaspoons chipotle peppers with adobo sauce (diced, if not using a food processor or blender)

Zest of 1 lime

Salt to taste

8 ears corn

For the butter, blend all the ingredients together in a food processor or beat with a fork. Form into little rosettes with a pastry bag, or form into a log and wrap it in parchment before chilling for 30 minutes or longer.

Remove husks and silks from the corn and carefully drop the ears into a large pot of boiling water. Bring the pot to a boil again and cook for 5 to 7 minutes. The pot of water should be large enough so the ears can float freely and so the water comes back to a boil within a few minutes. If there is too much corn in the water, it cooks poorly and takes a long time. Better to cook it in batches if you need to. Serve with the flavored butter.

SERVES 6–8

Needed in the Kitchen

—RAMANA LEWIS

When I assisted another cook, I baked cookies until my perspiration ran sticky with sugar and I smelled like butter and cinnamon. I tossed fat, green salads and served up gorgeous side dishes of plump fresh vegetables. I also assisted in other indispensable ways, like singing newly invented arias up past the rafters and starting water fights at the dish sink.

I was also a hindrance. The Tassajara kitchen bared the delicate, universal net of interconnectedness long before I was mature enough to stand responsibly and return to the kitchen with a bowlful of herbs.

One afternoon I was assisting Gloria Lee. The kitchen hummed obediently under her competent hand. Baking sheets mounded with cubed Yukon gold potatoes, slick with fragrant olive oil and gritty with salt and pepper, covered most of the available counters. The potatoes just needed a bouquet of fresh rosemary crumbled over them, and we would slide the trays into the oven to brown right before serving.

Gloria and I had just completed a winter practice period together at Green Gulch, and she was *shuso*, head student. I venerated her and felt entitled to her, like a possessive younger sister. Make no mistake: Gloria took no prisoners. But at least once a day I could make her blush and laugh by singing "G-L-O-R-I-A, Glo-ri-a!"

She moved deliberately and without waste. She tasted and stirred, checked her cookbook, wiped her forehead, and as serve-up came near, gave me a bowl to fill with rosemary from the garden. I tucked the bowl under my arm and vanished, leaving behind the concentrated order and responsibility of the kitchen. There was a lazy afternoon unfurling right outside. It enveloped me in contentment. My sense of time seeped away, and I simply enjoyed the aromatic herbs, my knees in the grass, the sun on my back.

A long time later I was startled. A blinding apron and long, tan legs filled my vision. I stood quickly, knowing something must be very wrong for Gloria to have left the stove. What could it be? Then it came to me.

"Where were you?" she demanded.

I braced for angry words. But she simply spread her fingers, palm up and began to cry. "I need you!"

I looked into her eyes and right down to human bedrock. The moment roared in my ears in pure heat, silencing the air. I was looking into her bones, and it ripped off my skin too. We both stood bare. I suddenly knew I would never be able to escape the consequences of being part of the whole. We were all in this together, like it or not.

I began to cry too and recognition passed between us. I saw my youth and her maturity in her face. Then she reached down and folded me in her long arms.

Pungent Cucumber Salad with Black Sesame and Ginger

This is a wonderful summer salad. You can also add shredded carrots with soaked, washed wakame. This is also quite nice on a bed of lettuce or arugula.

1 pound cucumbers, peeled, seeded, and cut into half moons, matchsticks, or chunks

$^1/_3$ teaspoon salt

4 tablespoons rice wine vinegar

1 tablespoon soy sauce

2 teaspoons mirin or $^1/_2$ tablespoon sugar

2 teaspoons grated ginger

$^1/_4$ to $^1/_2$ teaspoon red pepper flakes

1 teaspoon toasted black sesame seeds

Sprinkle cucumbers with salt; let drain in a colander over a bowl for at least 10 minutes. Mix together a simple dressing of vinegar, soy sauce, mirin, ginger, and red pepper flakes.

Give the cucumbers a gentle final squeeze to remove a little more water, dress them with the sweet vinegar mixture, and toss together with black sesame seeds. Chill before serving.

NOTE: *Salting the cucumbers and letting them sit helps draw out the water in their cell walls, which helps them soak up the dressing. Add just as much salt as you would normally use to season the cucumbers with. Some cucumber salad recipes let the cucumbers rest overnight to release all their liquid, but 30 minutes is usually sufficient, and a couple of hours is nice if you have the time. Try putting a weight on the cucumbers—sometimes the liquid draws more quickly. This is important for cucumber salads with creamy dressings because they often become too thin with the water from the cucumbers.*

SERVES 4–6

Mint Cilantro Chutney

Minty cool and refreshing, this spicy sweet chutney is a classic Indian condiment served with curries and dosas. It is also delicious as a sandwich spread.

1 jalapeño pepper, veins and seeds
   removed
³/₄ cup dried coconut
1 bunch fresh mint, stemmed
1 bunch fresh cilantro, stemmed

2 tablespoons honey
1 cup lime juice
¹/₂ teaspoon salt
Water

If using a food processor, drop the jalapeño into the bowl with the blade moving. Switch off the food processor and add the coconut to the bowl; chop for a few seconds. Add the mint and cilantro, and chop until fine. Add the remaining ingredients with enough water to make a sauce-like consistency. Refrigerate for a couple of hours or overnight to let the flavors develop.

SERVES 6–8

Raita

This traditional Indian dish is served with spicy curries, but is also nice as a soup with a squeeze of lemon.

1¹/₂ to 2 cups grated cucumber
1¹/₂ teaspoons salt
1 teaspoon cumin seeds

2 cups yogurt
Salt and pepper

Sprinkle cucumber with salt and let sit in a colander over a bowl for 20 minutes. Squeeze cucumbers, saving the juice if it is not bitter. If the cucumbers seem overly salty, rinse briefly with water.

Toast cumin seeds in a dry skillet just until you can smell the aroma.

Whisk the cucumber into the yogurt. Add cumin, salt, and pepper. If you saved the cucumber juice, add a little bit at a time until the raita is the consistency you like. If you run out of (or threw out) the cucumber juice, use a little lemon juice or milk to thin it out.

SERVES 4–6

Tamarind Chutney

Tamarind is a slightly sour paste made from a pulp that surrounds the seeds of a large tree. When buying tamarind at an Asian market, try to avoid the prepared jar paste and get the thick brown lump form that is wrapped in plastic. It keeps for months in the refrigerator.

3 tablespoons tamarind pulp

1 cup hot water for soaking tamarind

½ to 1 teaspoon salt

1 to 2 teaspoons sugar

½ teaspoon toasted and ground cumin

½ teaspoon toasted and ground coriander

½ teaspoon ground fennel seed

2 teaspoons grated ginger

Lemon juice

Chili powder

To make tamarind paste, soak the hard, sticky tamarind pulp in hot water for 10 to 15 minutes. Break up the pulp in the water, trying to separate the seeds from the tamarind. Put the tamarind in a fine sieve and force it through. You might need to use a little more water to help loosen it up before you can work the pulp through the strainer. Discard the seeds after harvesting as much pulp as you can. Combine the tamarind paste with all the remaining ingredients except the lemon juice and chili powder. Taste for salt and sugar, and add lemon juice to taste. Just a gentle squeeze of half a lemon can sometimes be enough to bring out the appropriate amount of sourness. A pinch of chili powder usually delivers the proper amount of heat. Let sit for a little while before adding more chili powder, because it will get hotter as it soaks into the chutney.

SERVES 4–6

"Some folks think that mindfulness means doing only one thing at a time. But I've found 'just this' while cooking means chopping and sautéing together. Mindfully chopping a carrot can certainly include paying attention to a certain prickle in the back of your neck that sends you over to the stove to stir the onions before you smell, too late, the scorched sauté."

—EVERETT WILSON

Daikon Salad with Lime-Ume Dressing

This is an unusual but deliciously refreshing cold salad to serve with sushi or tempura.

¹/₃ cup freshly squeezed lime juice

¹/₃ cup sugar

1 tablespoon ume plum paste or puréed
  umeboshi (pickled Japanese plums)

3 cups peeled daikon matchsticks

1¹/₂ cups peeled and grated carrots

Lettuce leaves

1 sheet nori, slivered (can cut with scissors
  to sliver)

Whisk together the lime juice, sugar, and ume paste. Toss with the daikon. For each serving, put a bed of grated carrots on a lettuce leaf, top with some daikon and dressing, and garnish with nori slivers. Serve immediately.

SERVES 4–6

Sweet Glazed Daikon

This recipe also works well with burdock root, which is incredibly energizing and cleansing. Carrots are also nice this way.

Sesame oil

4 cups daikon matchsticks

2 tablespoons mirin

2 tablespoons sake

Dashi or water as needed

2 teaspoons soy sauce

In a hot skillet, heat enough oil to generously coat the bottom of the pan. Sauté the daikon until it has softened and is beginning to brown. Add the mirin, sake, and enough dashi to come almost halfway up the vegetables. Cook over high heat until the liquid in the pan cooks down and almost evaporates, about 20 to 30 minutes. Add the soy sauce and taste to make sure the flavors balance each other nicely. Serve hot or cold as a main dish or as a condiment with *ohitashi,* a traditional Japanese salad of steamed or boiled vegetables arranged artfully on a plate.

SERVES 4–6

Sichuan Eggplant

Choose small shiny eggplants, as large eggplants can be quite bitter. If using a large eggplant, remove this bitterness by cutting up the eggplant and throwing in a few teaspoons of salt to coat its flesh. This draws out quite a bit of water and most of the bitterness. Let the salted eggplant sit in a colander over a bowl or on a cooling rack in a sheet pan. Rinse the salt off with a little water.

SAUCE

3 tablespoons Shaoxing rice wine or
    dry sherry

2 tablespoons soy sauce

1 to 2 tablespoons "rooster" sauce or other
    chili paste

2 teaspoons cider vinegar

$^1/_2$ teaspoon sugar

$^1/_2$ cup water or stock

EGGPLANT

2 to 3 tablespoons peanut oil

2 pounds eggplant, cut into 1-inch cubes

3 to 4 garlic cloves, minced

2 tablespoons minced fresh ginger (grated
    or cut into tiny slivers will also work)

$^1/_2$ cup thinly sliced scallions (sliced
    on a diagonal)

Salt

$^1/_2$ teaspoon sichuan peppercorns

1 to 2 tablespoons toasted sesame oil

To make the sauce, combine all the ingredients and set aside.

To make the eggplant, heat a wok or sauté pan and add oil. Wait until the oil shimmers; then add the eggplant and toss it to coat with oil. Add garlic, ginger, and scallions. Mix together and cook for 3 minutes, stirring occasionally to keep the eggplant from sticking to the pan. This develops a lot of flavor. The garlic, ginger, and scallions cook and flavor the oil that the eggplant soaks up.

Pour sauce into pan and stir well to get it nice and hot before covering. Reduce the heat to medium-low and simmer for 10 to 15 minutes, until the eggplant is tender and tasty. Taste for salt, pepper, and sesame oil. Best served hot and steaming from the wok, but it also makes a nice cold salad or room-temperature side dish.

For a nice variation, mix this eggplant with crumbled, oiled, and salted tofu baked on trays in the oven.

SERVES 4–6

Roasted Fennel and Radicchio

Nothing can replace the smoky anise flavor of grilled fennel or what a little wood smoke does for radicchio; but roasting things in the oven is so much more convenient because it requires little supervision. However you cook them, you'll enjoy the bitterness of the radicchio paired with the sweet caramelized fennel. Lay these out on a bed of baby greens for a beautiful composed salad.

3 to 4 fennel bulbs, sliced in 1-inch wedges
Olive oil
Salt and pepper

Balsamic vinegar (optional)
2 to 3 heads radicchio, sliced in
1-inch wedges

Toss the fennel with enough oil so that it is well coated. Sprinkle on a little salt and pepper, and spread out in single layers on sheet pans. Bake at 425 degrees for about 20 to 25 minutes. If the wedges begin to burn before getting soft and cooked through, turn the heat down to 350 degrees and bake them a little longer. If the fennel is not particularly sweet, drizzle on a little balsamic vinegar during the last 5 minutes of cooking time.

Toss the wedges of radicchio with oil and spread out on sheet pans. Add a little salt and pepper, and bake at 425 degrees for about 15 to 20 minutes, or until the leaves are tender and beginning to crisp up and darken. A few burned edges are nothing to worry about. People love them! Arrange fennel and radicchio on a platter, sprinkle with salt and pepper, and serve hot or cold.

NOTE: *Many people aren't quite sure how to approach a fennel bulb. If it comes with the greens attached, cut them off where they attach to the bulb and save them for stock. Unless your fennel is straight from the garden, you probably need to remove some of the outer layers of the bulb and a little slice of the dried-out root end. Slice off a sliver at the root end of the bulb if it looks dried up or brown. This may bring a few of the outer layers off with it. That's okay, chances are they also need to come off. Now you have this perfect little heart-like bulb. Cut the bulb in half and then cut angled sections (like an orange) that each have some of the core at their center. This makes them easy to flip when cooking, and then they can be arranged more beautifully when ready to serve.*

SERVES 4–6

Easy Greens with Soy Sauce and Honey

This recipe works well with any kind of cooked greens but is especially delicious with bitter greens like mustard.

1 bunch kale or mustard	1 to 2 teaspoons soy sauce
Oil	1 teaspoon honey
Water	

Carefully wash each leaf of kale or mustard in cold water. Stack as many leaves as you can on top of each other on a cutting board and gently roll them up together into a long cigar. This makes a nice tidy package to slice thin little pieces off all the leaves at once—a basic chiffonade. This is a very satisfying technique because you are left with a large pile of finely shredded greens. These thin pieces are much easier to digest. They require less chewing and provide more surface area for the sauce.

Heat a large skillet and add enough oil to generously coat the bottom of the pan. When the oil is hot, add the greens a few handfuls at a time to wilt them and to make enough room in the pan. Pour in just enough water to cover the bottom of the pan.

Cover the skillet with a lid and steam the greens for about 7 to 10 minutes, or just until softened. Uncover the pan and add a splash or two of soy sauce and the honey. Stir over heat to combine and continue to cook for a minute or two to boil off some of the water in order to thicken the sauce.

SERVES 4–6

Kashmiri-Style Greens with Roasted Potatoes

Any kind of greens work well in this dish. Collards work well for crowds because they do not cook down quite as much. The quantities for potatoes are not exact. They can either be used as a garnish or as a more substantial element for bulk.

2 cups medium-chopped potatoes
2 tablespoons vegetable oil, plus more for
    sautéing
Salt and pepper

1 teaspoon mustard seeds
1 pinch asafoetida (*hing* in Chinese)
1 serrano pepper, minced
1 head fresh greens, finely chopped

Roast potatoes in 2 tablespoons oil, salt, and pepper at 425 degrees until crisp and cooked, about 45 minutes. They should be succulent inside and have a golden brown surface.

Heat additional oil in a sauté pan with the mustard seeds. When seeds begin to pop, add asafoetida. Let this sizzle for 5 seconds and then add the serrano pepper.

Toss the pepper once; then add greens and sauté quickly. Cook until done, about 15 minutes for a small quantity but much longer if you have to cook large quantities. If your pot isn't big enough, just cook what fits and keep adding more as it cooks down. Toss in warm potatoes right at the end.

SERVES 4–6

Crispy Baked Kale

This is a great way to eat greens—they are almost like potato chips. This cooking technique helps keep the greens from losing all their volume. Sometimes less really is more.

1 large bunch kale
2 to 3 tablespoons olive oil

Salt and freshly ground black pepper

Preheat oven to 350 degrees. Wash and dry the kale, and then tear the stems from the leaves. Toss with oil and bake in a single layer on sheet pans until crisp around the edges of the leaves, about 10 to 12 minutes. Season with salt and pepper. Serve hot or cold.

SERVES 4

Ginger Apricot Chutney

This chutney can be kept in a sterilized jar in the refrigerator for months.

2 tablespoons ghee or coconut oil
1 (3-inch) cinnamon stick
¼ teaspoon cardamom seeds
½ pound dried apricots, soaked in 2 cups
    hot water for 15 to 20 minutes
½ teaspoon black sesame seeds
½ tablespoon grated ginger

⅔ cup raisins or currants
½ cup brown sugar (optional)
¼ to ½ teaspoon salt
2 to 3 tablespoons apple cider vinegar
⅛ to ¼ teaspoon cayenne pepper (watch
    out—it gets MUCH hotter as it cooks
    and even hotter the next day)

Heat a heavy-bottom pot or saucepan over medium-high heat. Add the ghee and then sauté the cinnamon and cardamom for 1 to 2 minutes until it begins to get fragrant. Put the apricots with their soaking liquid, sesame seeds, ginger, raisins, and sugar into the pot, and bring to a boil. Turn the heat down to low and simmer until thickened. Season with salt, vinegar, and cayenne pepper.

SERVES 6–8

Crispy Baked Kale

Stir-Fried Pea Shoots

Pea shoots are sweet and flavorful. If you are lucky enough to find them, this is a favorite stir-fry. Pea shoots are the young curly tendrils of a pea plant but most often come from snow peas. They are sometimes grown to be sold as pea shoots and are a real treat. Well worth starting a garden for!

Oil	1 pound pea shoots, washed and cut in half
1 to 2 garlic cloves, minced	if longer than 6 inches
	Salt and pepper

Heat a wok or a skillet and add a few tablespoons of oil over high heat; add the garlic and toss for a few seconds to flavor the oil. Throw in pea shoots and stir-fry quickly until the shoots are bright green and tender, no more than a few minutes. Salt and pepper to taste. Serve hot or as a nice cool salad.

SERVES 4–6

Very Aware

—EVA TUSCHMAN

I remain immensely grateful for the practice opportunity of being guest cook, because it was the first time in my life I learned to completely trust my strong intuitive sense. Leaping into the unknown, with no time to lose, there I was—responding, stirring, smelling, tasting—with every capacity I had. It was a true gift to be able to create with such abundance, providing nourishing and aesthetically pleasing offerings for the guests.

"I was very aware throughout the season how much I was carried through the entire experience by so many others: upon entering the kitchen each day, I felt as if I was merely a participant in something much larger or greater than myself. I think that to feel this profound interconnectedness is the mystery, joy, and beauty of the Tassajara summer kitchen.

Moroxican Spiced Potatoes

It is probably no coincidence that Morocco and Mexico share so many spices and flavors. Cumin, coriander, and garlic make these crisp, brown, oven-fried potatoes a delicious side dish for almost any equatorial cuisine. These go well with mushroom ragout or tossed with steamed greens.

1½ pounds potatoes, cut into
   1-inch chunks
1 head garlic, cloves separated
   but not peeled

Olive oil
1½ teaspoons cumin seeds
1½ teaspoons coriander seeds, ground
Salt and pepper to taste

Toss potatoes and garlic with the oil, cumin, coriander, salt, and pepper. Roast at 425 degrees in a single layer in an oiled baking dish for about 30 minutes, or until soft when pierced with a knife. Shake or stir the potatoes regularly to keep them from sticking and to make sure they brown evenly. If they are stuck to the pan, don't force them free. Put them back in the oven for 5 minutes and then try to release them. There is a certain point in forming a crust that the starchy potatoes get cemented to the pan. When a nice brown crust has formed, they should release easily.

SERVES 4–6

Roasted Fingerling Potatoes and Corn in Dijon Vinaigrette

The multiple varieties of fingerling heirloom potatoes—such as Purple Peruvian, Yellow Finn, and Rose Finn Apple, among others—make their appearance at farmers markets beginning in spring. Each type has a slightly different texture, flavor, and color, but all are delicious when roasted. Make this simple side dish when fresh corn reaches its peak as part of a midsummer evening picnic.

POTATOES AND CORN

2 pounds fingerling potatoes

Extra virgin olive oil

Coarse salt and pepper

4 ears corn

$1/8$ cup rough chiffonade of fresh tarragon leaves

VINAIGRETTE

1 tablespoon Dijon mustard

$1/3$ cup red wine vinegar

Splash of champagne vinegar

1 tablespoon fresh lemon juice

$3/4$ cup extra virgin olive oil

To make the potatoes, heat the oven to 400 degrees. Scrub the potatoes and slice them in half lengthwise. (If they are very large, you may wish to quarter them.) Lightly brush the potatoes with the oil and dust with salt and pepper. Place on a baking dish and roast until tender, about 40 minutes.

The corn can roast simultaneously, although it does not take too long for the natural sugars to be released. Shave the corn kernels from the cobs and toss them lightly in a bowl with oil. Arrange in a single layer on a baking tray and roast for 15 to 20 minutes, or until the corn becomes juicy.

To make the vinaigrette, whisk the mustard, vinegars, and lemon juice together. Whisk in the oil. While the potatoes are still warm from the oven, toss them with the corn, vinaigrette, and tarragon leaves. Add salt and pepper to taste.

SERVES 6–8

Spinach with Sesame

It may seem like a lot of spinach, but once blanched and pressed of its water, spinach wilts considerably. Serve this refreshing salad cold or at room temperature with soba noodles or other Japanese dishes. The sesame sauce keeps well for up to three weeks in the refrigerator and is delicious with other vegetables.

$1\frac{1}{2}$ pounds fresh spinach leaves

Salt

4 tablespoons sesame seeds, black or tan
   (save $\frac{1}{2}$ teaspoon for garnish)

$\frac{1}{4}$ cup water or vegetable stock

1 tablespoon honey

1 teaspoon soy sauce

1 tablespoon rice wine vinegar

2 teaspoons miso

You may wish to remove the stems of the spinach if they are long and tough.

Meanwhile, bring a large pot of water to a boil. Add several teaspoons of salt. (Blanching vegetables, particularly greens or broccoli, in salty ocean-like water helps to maintain their radiant color.) Once the water has boiled, quickly immerse the spinach and allow it to wilt for just 30 seconds. Retrieve the spinach with tongs and place in a colander. Wash immediately with cold water to prevent overcooking. In small batches, squeeze the spinach between your hands, wringing it of excess water. You may be surprised by how much water it releases. Continue to press the water from the leaves until you have small compressed mounds.

In a small saucepan over low heat, toast the sesame seeds until they release their fragrance and oil. It is traditional in Japan to use a *suribachi,* or an unglazed clay mortar with grooves, to grind sesame seeds for this sauce. A smooth mortar can substitute, although it is less effective. Alternatively, using a food processor, pulse the sesame seeds until they form a rough paste, leaving some of the seeds still intact. Gradually add the water to help in this process. Follow with the honey, soy sauce, vinegar, and miso until the sauce is fully integrated. You may wish to add more liquid to adjust the consistency. Taste for salt and sugar, and correct as needed.

Coat the spinach thoroughly and evenly with the sauce and mound the greens on a serving dish; sprinkle with a few extra toasted sesame seeds.

SERVES 4

Ginger Mashed Yams

This is a lovely dish that takes very little effort once the yams are washed and chopped. Butter is optional if you want to cut the fat or serve a vegan dish.

1 (14-ounce) can coconut milk

$^1/_4$ cup butter

1 tablespoon brown sugar

$^1/_2$ teaspoon salt

$^1/_2$ cup minced ginger

5 yams, peeled or unpeeled, cut into $^3/_4$-inch cubes

Candied ginger, finely diced

Cover and cook all ingredients over medium-low heat until yams are tender, stirring occasionally. Remove from heat and mash with a potato masher. Garnish with candied ginger.

SERVES 4–6

Roasted Yams with Ancho Chile Paste

If you use garnet yams, the orange color is the perfect background for the deep reddish brown of the chile sauce. The tastes are similarly complementary, with the sweet yam being the ideal vehicle for the earthy heat of the roasted chiles.

8 to 12 dried ancho chiles

Boiling water

4 garlic cloves

1 teaspoon epazote or Mexican oregano

$^1/_2$ teaspoon cinnamon

2 tablespoons olive oil

1 cup water or stock

8 cups yams, cut lengthwise like steak fries

Toast the chiles over an open flame or in a cast-iron pan over high heat for a few seconds per side. Remove the stems and seeds, and soak the toasted chiles in the hot water until they are soft and plump, about 10 minutes. Drain the chiles and blend with garlic, epazote, cinnamon, oil, and water. Coat the yams with the chile sauce and bake at 350 degrees until cooked through, about 30 minutes.

SERVES 6–8

Roasted Winter Squash

Winter squash can be a little intimidating to prep the first time. Just use your biggest knife and be careful.

1 winter squash, cut in half, seeded, and cut into 1-inch squares	Oil Salt

Preheat oven to 450 degrees. Brush squash with mild oil, like canola or sunflower, and sprinkle with salt. Bake until browned but not overcooked. Serve at room temperature with Sesame Vinegar Dressing or Sesame Miso Dressing (see page 203).

SERVES 4–6

Roasted Zucchini with Garlic Oil

Almost every summer there is at least one guest cook who loves to spend the afternoon outside the kitchen in "the pit," playing with fire and grilling piles of fresh zucchini. While there is nothing quite like eating a perfectly grilled zucchini, this recipe offers a fair substitute without having to light a fire.

5 medium zucchini, halved lengthwise 3 to 4 tablespoons Garlic Oil (see page 204)	Salt and freshly ground black pepper

Preheat the oven to 450 degrees. With a paring knife, score the cut surface of the zucchini in a cross-hatched pattern. This helps the heat get into the heart of the zucchini and gives extra surface area for the oil to seep into. Place zucchini, cut side down, on a lightly oiled sheet pan; brush with the Garlic Oil. Bake for 15 to 20 minutes, or until the squash is getting soft and the skin in contact with the pan is brown and beginning to blacken. Season with salt and pepper, and serve warm or cold.

SERVES 4–6

vegetable entrées

James Creek Farm Ratatouille

All summer long Tassajara benefits from the work of John Kinder at James Creek Farm. His farm is in the heart of the Ventana Wilderness and throughout the summer we eat all that he can grow!

2 tablespoons olive oil	4 cups cubed eggplant (1-inch cubes)
1 cup chopped onion	2 cups cubed bell peppers (1-inch squares)
1 teaspoon dried marjoram or oregano	2 or 3 thick slices summer squash
½ teaspoon dried rosemary	4 cups peeled, seeded, and chopped tomatoes
½ teaspoon salt	1 bay leaf
2 tablespoons minced garlic	¼ cup chopped fresh basil

Heat a large skillet and add the oil. Sauté the onion, herbs, and salt over medium-high heat until soft and beginning to brown. Add the garlic and cook for 1 minute before adding the eggplant and bell peppers. Cook 10 minutes, or until vegetable are getting tender. Add the squash, tomatoes, and bay leaf. Stew over low heat until the squash is tender and the flavors have all come together, about 20 to 30 minutes. Taste for salt and pepper, stir in the fresh basil, and serve.

SERVES 6–8

The Tenzo Said

—EIHEI DOGEN

When I was at Tiantong Temple, a person named Yong from Qingyuan Prefecture had the job of tenzo. I happened to be passing through the eastern corridor after lunch when the tenzo was drying mushrooms in front of the Buddha hall. He carried a bamboo cane but had no hat on his head. The sun beat down on the hot pavement, and the sweat flowed down and drenched him as he resolutely dried the mushrooms. I saw he was struggling a bit. With his spine bent like a bow and his shaggy eyebrows, he looked like a crane.

I approached and politely asked the tenzo his age. He said he was sixty-eight.

I asked, "Why do you not have an attendant or lay worker do this?"

The tenzo said, "What time should I wait for?"

I immediately withdrew. Thinking to myself as I walked away, I deeply appreciated that this job [expresses] the essential function.

Mushroom Ragout

This recipe describes a classic French technique called monter au beurre *in which small pieces of cold butter are quickly emulsified into a hot liquid. When done correctly, the butter is turned back into cream and the sauce is smooth and velvety. These types of sauces can break, or fall out of emulsion, into an ugly mixture of water and fat if they get too hot (above 135 to 140 degrees) or too cool (below body temperature). You can usually fix a broken sauce by whisking in a little more butter, some heavy cream, or a few tablespoons of cold water.*

1 tablespoon olive oil
1½ yellow onions, medium-chopped
½ teaspoon salt
2 tablespoons minced garlic
1½ tablespoons dry Italian herbs
    (oregano, basil, thyme, savory,
    and rosemary)
2 pinches freshly ground black pepper
1 cup dry white wine

1 teaspoon soy sauce (mushroom soy
    sauce, if available)
4 cups quartered button mushrooms
4 cups quartered crimini mushrooms
1 cup sliced shiitake mushrooms
    (¼-inch slices)
1 cup stock
2 to 4 tablespoons cold butter, thinly sliced
2 tablespoons chopped parsley

Heat the oil in a large sauté pan. Add the onions and salt, and cook over medium-high heat until the onions soften, release their juices, and begin to brown. Add the garlic, dry herbs, and pepper, and cook for 30 seconds more, stirring constantly. Add the wine and soy sauce, turn the heat down to medium-low, and let simmer for about 7 minutes, or until the mixture has reduced and slightly thickened and the alcohol has burned off.

Turn the heat back up to medium-high while adding the mushrooms, which should release their juices in just a couple of minutes, during which time you should stir once or twice. If it looks like they are going to burn before releasing their juices, feel free to add the stock in part or whole. If not, add the stock when the juices have begun to be released.

Turn the heat down to medium-low and let the dish simmer at least 20 minutes and up to 1 hour or more. When you are ready to serve, turn the heat off and add the butter a slice or two at a time while stirring constantly. When all the butter has melted and is fully mixed, serve over polenta squares, potatoes, or pasta. Garnish with the chopped parsley.

SERVES 4–6

Vegetable Tempura (Shojin Age)

Vegetables have so many combinations of textures, colors, and flavors. Let your imagination guide you, but, of course, almost anything tastes good when it is battered and deep-fried.

2 cups very cold water
2 eggs
2 cups all-purpose or whole wheat flour

Enough oil to fill a pot 2 to 3 inches deep
About 8 cups cut-up or thinly sliced
   vegetables (see note)

Mix the water and eggs together. Sprinkle the flour over the liquid and stir quickly with a whisk. Be careful not to overmix the batter or it will be tough and heavy.

Heat the oil (sesame, safflower, or rice bran oil) in a heavy pot to 345 to 355 degrees. If the oil is at the right temperature, a small piece of batter will sink to the bottom of the pan and float to the top quickly. If it stays at the bottom, the oil is not hot enough. If the piece of dropped batter never sinks and just floats immediately, the temperature is too high. If the oil smokes, the temperature is way too high. When the oil is the right temperature, dredge the vegetables in the batter and cook a few at a time until golden. Frying too many pieces at once lowers the oil temperature. Cook the first side for about 1 minute and then turn over with chopsticks, tongs, or a long fork to brown the other side. Depending on the cut of the vegetables, each piece should cook about 2 to 3 minutes.

A simple sauce made with a few tablespoons of soy sauce, dashi,* a little grated ginger, and maybe some mirin is nice for dipping.

NOTE: *Slice denser vegetables like carrots and yams thin enough so that they cook through quickly. Tempura is traditionally served with a little grated daikon and ginger to help soak up and digest the oil.*

*Dashi is a simple kombu stock prepared by simmering a 3-inch piece of kombu in a few cups of water or by soaking it overnight in cool spring water. Kombu is a leathery dried seaweed found in Asian markets and many grocery stores. It adds subtle flavor to many Japanese soups and sauces.

SERVES 4–6

Vegetables in Thai Red Curry

With the availability of great prepared Thai curries, this dish is very easy to make.

1 small head cauliflower, cut into florets

1 cup green beans, stems removed and
   cut into 2 inch pieces

1 tablespoon canola oil

1 cup crimini mushrooms, ends trimmed
   (left whole if small, quartered if large)

1 (14-ounce) can coconut milk

½ cup water

1 to 2 tablespoons Thai red curry paste

2 tablespoons brown sugar

2 tablespoons tamari

1 small sweet red pepper, cored, seeded,
   and cut into slivers

20 to 30 fresh Thai basil leaves, whole

In a pot of boiling salted water, blanch the cauliflower to al dente, about 4 minutes. Rinse under cold water to stop the cooking. In the same pot of water, repeat with the green beans; set aside. In a sauté pan, add the oil and cook the mushrooms until they're browned and have released some juices; set aside.

In a wide saucepan, add the coconut milk, water, curry paste, sugar, and tamari. Start with a small amount of curry paste and then taste for spiciness. Add the cauliflower, green beans, mushrooms, red pepper, and half of the basil. Simmer for 10 minutes. Garnish with remaining basil and serve with jasmine rice.

SERVES 4–6

Learning to Work Faster

—MEG LEVIE

The first summer I was a guest cook, I had been in the kitchen at Tassajara for only one practice period, so I had a lot to learn. I was very fortunate that my cooking partner was Ryn Wood, who had learned to cook at Greens Restaurant and later went on to start her own restaurant in Sebastopol. She taught me a lot, but I found the first couple of months to be a real challenge. I didn't know if I could learn enough to be ready to cook for the peak guest season; but finally, after two months of really hard work and lots of help, I thought, "I can do this now."

A couple of days later I was in the kitchen with Ryn and she suggested we go up to the storage loft because she said she needed to talk to me. She looked at me seriously but kindly and said, "Meg, you have to learn to work faster. I'm having to cover for you too much and I can't keep it up." I was devastated. I stayed up there and cried for a while. And then I learned to work faster.

Sweet and Sour Vegetables with Deep-Fried Walnuts

This is a fun vegetarian version of a classic Chinese-American restaurant dish. In China it is traditional to have a sweet and sour dish to celebrate the new year.

DEEP-FRIED WALNUTS

½ cup cornstarch

½ cup all-purpose flour

¼ teaspoon ground white or black pepper

2 tablespoons soy sauce

½ cup water

1½ cups walnuts

Peanut oil

SAUCE

1 tablespoon soy sauce

¼ cup ketchup

2 tablespoons sugar

¼ cup white rice vinegar (or any vinegar you have)

½ cup pineapple juice (drained from the pineapple chunks)

2 tablespoons minced or grated ginger

3 to 4 garlic cloves, minced

1 tablespoon cornstarch

STIR-FRY

1½ cups cubed onions (1-inch cubes)

1½ cups roughly chopped or thinly sliced mushrooms

1½ cups cubed bell peppers (1-inch squares), different colors are nice

1½ cups chopped carrots (¾-inch dice)

1 (20-ounce) can pineapple chunks (see note)

4 scallions, thinly sliced

To make the walnuts, mix together the cornstarch, flour, and pepper. Whisk in soy sauce and water. Coat walnuts in batter. Deep-fry the walnuts in the oil heated to 365 degrees. Drain on paper towels and pat down to soak up the oil. The batter is very sticky and thick. Be careful to drop the walnuts into the oil one at a time so that they don't just form one large clump. If they do start sticking together, go ahead and let the whole mess brown and then break it up when cool. Re-batter and fry as needed.

To make the sauce, mix together the soy sauce, ketchup, sugar, vinegar, and pineapple juice. In a small saucepan, sauté the ginger and garlic. Add all the ingredients except the cornstarch to the ginger and garlic (if you just put the cornstarch in straight, it will clump) and simmer until the sugar dissolves. When it is nice and hot, thicken with a cornstarch slurry. (Make a smooth slurry by mixing cornstarch with a little hot liquid in a separate bowl.) Set the sauce aside.

For the stir-fry, heat oil over high heat and add the vegetables. When the carrots are getting soft and the onions are nicely translucent, pour the sauce over the vegetables and simmer for a few minutes to let the flavors marry. Stir in pineapple and scallions, and continue cooking until warmed through. Stir in the fried walnuts and serve immediately.

NOTE: *Canned pineapple chunks are optional but the juice is really nice to have. If you don't want to use pineapple, try substituting orange juice with a squeeze of lemon or lime in its place.*

SERVES 6–8

What's That Smell?

—JESSE WEINS

It never fails: everything can seem to be going exceedingly well; you're thrilled with how the flavor of the stew came out, all the dishes are being finished ahead of schedule, and there's still plenty of time before serve up; so, you think, it's a perfect time to relax . . . when suddenly, you hear someone by the stove asking "what's that smell?" Time stops with the realization that your oh-so-perfect stew is burning! Calamity! The stew's once-in-a-lifetime flavor, which you worked so hard to achieve, is ruined! Several minutes of fiddling tells you that no amount of added ingredients can mask the taste of carbon. You're out of time. Eyes downcast, shoulders hunched in apprehension, you send the burnt stew off to the paying guests. You slink off to your own meal chased by visions of angry mobs with pitchforks.

Then a funny thing happens: praise starts bubbling out of the dining room. The servers return with the best complement a cook can ask for, "The guests want to know, how'd you make that stew? What's the secret ingredient?" Suddenly, your shoulders relax and that stew starts to taste alright to your tongue. Your brain starts to shift gears. Angry villagers are replaced by cheering crowds. Hey, maybe you're not such a terrible cook—in fact, isn't it the great cooks who turn their mistakes into masterpieces?

Of course, great cooks wouldn't give away all their secrets. So, you point the server to the *Tassajara Cookbook*. "The recipe's in there. They can buy it in the bookstore." The server smiles, having heard that answer every night, and disappears back into the darkness. Cheers fade, the bubbling creek returns, and once more, all is well.

Tagine with Apricots, Olives, and Artichoke Hearts

Tagine refers to the fragrant and juicy North African dish of slowly simmered vegetables. This version highlights the height of summer produce: new potatoes, eggplant, tomatoes, green beans, and red peppers. During other times of the year, seasonally appropriate vegetables can be substituted. Serve over a steaming bed of couscous tossed with dried cherries and toasted slivered almonds.

Oil
6 to 8 new potatoes, quartered
Salt
1 globe eggplant, cut in half lengthwise,
    then into ½-inch half-moons
4 tablespoons extra virgin olive oil
2 red onions, thinly sliced
1½ teaspoons ground cumin
1½ teaspoons ground cinnamon
1 teaspoon turmeric
1 teaspoon ground saffron
2 red bell peppers, seeded, ribbed, and cut
    lengthwise into narrow strips

Vegetable stock as needed
1 tablespoon tomato paste
2 teaspoons honey
¼ pound green beans, stemmed and cut
    in half diagonally
4 fresh ripe tomatoes, roughly chopped
6 artichoke hearts
½ cup slivered dried Turkish apricots
    (unsulfured)
¼ cup pitted kalamata or other black olives
Handful of fresh Italian or flat-leaf parsley,
    roughly chopped
Handful of cilantro leaves, roughly chopped

Preheat the oven to 400 degrees. Lightly oil the potatoes and roast for 30 minutes in a baking dish until soft when pierced with a fork. Lightly salt the eggplant and allow to sweat for 20 minutes. Wipe off moisture, spray with water, and pat dry.

Warm the olive oil over medium heat and wilt the onions until they are translucent. Add the spices, stirring frequently. Add the eggplant, bell peppers, and some stock to prevent the vegetables from burning. When the eggplant begins to soften, add the tomato paste, honey, green beans, potatoes, tomatoes, and artichoke hearts. Add the apricots and olives, simmering over low heat, and add more stock as needed to create a rich sauce. The tagine can cook like this for several hours and the vegetables become infused with the spices—but do not overcook the vegetables to the point of disintegration.

Once the sauce thickens, taste for seasonings and adjust as needed. Stir in the parsley and cilantro leaves, reserving some for garnish. Eat with pita bread to absorb the delicious juices left on your plate. The tagine will be even better the next day as the flavors have time to truly mingle.

SERVES 6–8

Coconut Curry with Mixed Vegetables

This curry is always popular and it is a wonderful introduction to the flavors of India. As with most stews, it is even better the second day.

2 tablespoons vegetable oil or ghee
1 tablespoon brown mustard seeds
2 cups diced onions
2 tablespoons minced garlic
2 tablespoons minced ginger
1½ tablespoons Garam Masala (see page 207)

1 (14-ounce) can diced tomatoes (or use fresh)
4 cups cooked vegetables (potatoes, carrots, greens, mushrooms, etc.)
1 lemon, juiced
1 (14-ounce) can coconut milk
½ cup toasted cashews

Heat oil in pan over medium-high heat. When the oil starts to shimmer, add the mustard seeds. When the seeds begin to pop, add the onions. When the onions are soft, add the garlic, ginger, and Garam Masala. Stir briefly, then add the tomatoes and simmer for as long as you can. This is the curry base and now any sort of cooked vegetables can be added.

Add the cooked vegetables to the curry base. Simmer for about 30 minutes so the flavors come together. If it is too sour, add some sugar, but it should not be sweet. Add the lemon juice and coconut milk just before serving and heat—do not boil. Garnish with the cashews.

NOTE: *Roast oiled carrots, potatoes, and yams in a hot oven for 15 to 20 minutes. Roast whole mushrooms on a dry sheet pan until brown. Steam or blanch vegetables so they've still got some crunch, about 4 minutes. They should still be squeaky to the tooth, or else they'll overcook in the final cooking that's coming up.*

Traditionally you might sauté all of the vegetables separately in ghee and some of the Garam Masala, but that's not really worth the trouble.

Curry just means "sauce." Pay attention to the tomato curry base every step of the way. Try to build flavor with each step, but don't let anything burn or the stew will be bitter. Unlike other fruits and vegetables, tomatoes and onions benefit from a long afternoon of stewing with their spices.

SERVES 4–6

baked entrées

Pizza with Pesto, Ricotta, and Heirloom Tomatoes 89

Fresh Corn, Red Pepper, and Spinach Timbale 91

Mushroom Galette 92

Goat Cheese Enchilada Pie with Kale and Potatoes 94

Baked Muffaletta Crêpes 95

Tofu Lasagna with Mushrooms, Goat Cheese, and Chard 96

Annie's Frittata with Caramelized Onions, Goat Cheese, and Sage 99

Stuffed Peppers with Pine Nuts, Apricots, and Mint 100

Pizza with Pesto, Ricotta, and Heirloom Tomatoes

This pizza represents Tassajara's approach to pizza making. The richness of the pesto is complemented by the creaminess of the ricotta, and if you happen to get some true vine-ripened heirloom tomatoes as we do from James Creek Farms at the end of summer, you truly will have a treat. We made this pizza with a tomato sauce and mozzarella, but it could easily be made without tomato sauce for a lighter touch.

Pizza Dough (see page 154)
Cornmeal or flour
Roasted Tomato Sauce, cooked down
    until very thick (see page 210)
12 ounces mozzarella cheese, grated

Fresh Basil Pesto (see page 211)
12 ounces ricotta cheese
6 to 8 heirloom tomatoes, sliced
Rosemary Garlic Oil (see page 204)
Kosher salt

Preheat oven to 500 degrees.

Roll out or stretch the pizza dough to the desired shape. Dust the baking sheet with flour or sprinkle it with coarse cornmeal. Place the dough on the pan. Add a thin layer of tomato sauce to within ½ inch of the edge. Sprinkle with mozzarella. Add the pesto and ricotta in dollops. Bake until edges are golden brown. Take the pizza out of the oven and place the tomato slices on top. Brush the edges with the Rosemary Garlic Oil and sprinkle lightly with salt.

NOTE: *Making pizza for the masses at Tassajara is always a little stressful. It starts with making 30 pounds of pizza dough and dividing this into 30 perfect one-pound rounds. Then you roll out all the rounds into flat circles and try to find space for all the pizzas you are working with. After you have the rounds rolled out, you can start topping them with the toppings that you prepared earlier. When there were a lot of families living at Tassajara, the kids would come in and help top the pizzas. Your pizza parties at home can start well before the pies are even out of the oven.*

Help! The Pizzas Are Burning!

—MARY MOCINE

After 6 hours of continuous pizza-making action, I was finally getting a few minutes to rest. My middle-aged body was exhausted. A kind fellow cook started to give me a neck rub. All of a sudden I smelled them. The pizzas were burning.

"HELP!" I cried out, "My pizzas are burning! I need them out of the oven . . . right NOW!"

Luckily the crew was just coming back from student dinner. Chris Hamburger, the *fukaten* (kitchen work leader), led the charge. From all directions people descended upon the twelve pizzas, and they were out of the oven in a matter of seconds.

It was one of those times when the kitchen crew became so much more than the sum of its parts. A good crew can learn to move like one body with one brain. Gathered around the center counter with everyone clearing space and moving things around together, the crew becomes a many-handed deity pulling the pizzas out of the oven and slicing them up with knives and rolling blades. It is easy to feel the truth of interdependence when you share moments like these.

Fresh Corn, Red Pepper, and Spinach Timbale

This savory vegetable custard is particularly beautiful, but timbales can be made with just about any cooked vegetable. The Greens Cookbook (2001) by Deborah Madison and Edward Espe Brown, has some wonderful ideas for timbales. Let your imagination and the bounty of your garden or the farmers market guide you. A timbale can also turn any sort of leftovers into an elegant easy-to-prepare dish.

Butter	1 cup corn (from about 2 ears)
1 pound cooked spinach, finely chopped	1 red bell pepper, finely chopped
1½ cups milk	½ cup grated cheese
3 eggs	2 tablespoons grated Parmesan cheese
Salt and pepper	(optional)

Preheat the oven to 350 degrees.

Butter a 1-quart casserole dish. Make sure to squeeze as much liquid out of the spinach as possible. Whisk together the milk and eggs, and then stir in the remaining ingredients except the Parmesan cheese. Pour the mixture into the dish and sprinkle the Parmesan over the top. Bake for about 45 minutes, or until the custard has set and the top is a little browned.

NOTE: *For the best texture, bake in a bain-marie or a water bath, which is simply a baking dish filled with enough hot water to come halfway up the side of the casserole. This helps transfer the heat of the oven in a very even, gentle way so that the custard comes out with a silky smooth texture.*

SERVES 4–6

Mushroom Galette

This filling can go into Buckwheat Crêpes (see page 152) for a nice wheat-free alternative to the rich crust of the galette.

1 cup chopped onion
3 cups thinly sliced fresh mushrooms
2 tablespoons herbes de Provence
1 teaspoon salt
½ to 1 cup white wine
1 bunch hardy greens, stemmed (kale, mustard, etc.)

Simple and Delicious Yeasted Tart Dough (see page 150)
4 tablespoons grated Parmesan or cheddar cheese
6 ounces goat cheese

Sauté onion until translucent. Add the mushrooms, herbs, and salt, and cook for 15 to 20 minutes, or longer if the volume is large. The mushrooms should release their juices, filling the pan with liquid. Add the wine and cook down until the mushrooms are brown and the mixture begins to caramelize. Steam greens until cooked and put in a colander to drain.

Roll out dough and place on a sheet pan. Sprinkle the Parmesan or cheddar in the middle. This melts and forms a watertight seal that helps keep the crust crisp.

Squeeze as much water as you can out of the greens and then chop. Toss with goat cheese and mushrooms. Put mixture in middle of dough, then fold up the sides to form the galette. Bake at 425 degrees for 15 minutes, then turn the oven down to 350 degrees and bake another 15 to 30 minutes. It is done when the crust is brown and the insides are bubbling. The bottom of the crust should be golden, crisp, and dry.

SERVES 4–6

Goat Cheese Enchilada Pie with Kale and Potatoes

Enchiladas can be rolled or stacked. At Tassajara, we tend to make stacked enchiladas because of the labor involved in rolling them. They taste just as delicious!

3 cups chopped potatoes
1 cup chopped carrots
1 head kale, stemmed (about a pound)
2 cups thinly sliced onions
Oil
15 to 20 corn tortillas

1 cup crumbled goat cheese
Salt and pepper
3 to 6 cups Roasted Tomato Sauce (see page 210), Easy Red Mole (see page 216), or tomatillo salsa
½ cup grated Monterey Jack cheese (optional)

Blanch potatoes and carrots separately in a little water for about 10 minutes. They should still be al dente, as they will cook a bit more while the enchiladas bake. You can use the cooking water in the sauce if you like.

Steam kale for about 10 minutes. Let it cool naturally or shock it in a bowl of cold water. You just need to be able to handle it comfortably. Roughly chop the leaves and squeeze out as much liquid as you can. Let rest in a colander to drain until needed.

Sauté the onions quickly over high heat with a little oil for about 10 to 20 minutes.

If you are rolling the enchiladas, mix the vegetables and the goat cheese together in a large bowl with salt and pepper. If you are stacking your enchiladas, you are ready to start assembling right away.

Oil a deep casserole dish and put a little sauce in the bottom. Lay a tortilla down then a little bit of each of the vegetables. Sprinkle a little goat cheese over this first layer and finish by covering with a few tablespoons of sauce. Lay down another tortilla to start the next layer. Continue until you run out of filling. End with a final tortilla smothered with sauce. Sprinkle the optional cheese over the top and bake at 350 degrees until warmed through and beginning to bubble around the edges, about 30 minutes.

SERVES 6–8

Baked Muffaletta Crêpes

This delicious recipe was inspired by a famous sandwich from New Orleans that was probably invented in 1906 at the Central Grocery by Salvatore Lupo, a Sicilian emigrant. Muffaletta is actually the name of the focaccia-like bread the sandwich is served on but has come to be used to also refer to the sandwich made with a pickled olive and cauliflower salad, sandwich meats, and cheese. These crêpes filled with zesty cauliflower, olives, and capers capture something of the classic New Orleans sandwich.

2 to 3 tablespoons olive oil
1 cup thinly sliced onion
½ cup diced celery
½ cup diced carrots
½ teaspoon salt
1 teaspoon dried oregano
4 garlic cloves, minced
2 cups finely chopped cauliflower florets
½ cup roughly chopped green olives with pimientos

½ cup roughly chopped black olives
2 tablespoons capers
2 to 3 tablespoons pickling juice from capers or olives
Freshly ground black pepper
8 Buckwheat Crêpes (see page 152)
3 to 4 cups Creamy Saffron Tomato Sauce (see page 211)
1 to 2 cups grated provolone cheese

Heat a large sauté pan over high heat. Pour in the oil and let heat for about 1 minute. Sauté the onion, celery, carrots, salt, and oregano until vegetables are softened, about 7 minutes. Add the garlic and cauliflower, and continue cooking until the cauliflower is beginning to lose its crunch, about 5 minutes. Add olives and capers with the juice and continue cooking just to heat through. Season with pepper. The filling benefits from a night in the refrigerator but you may use it right away.

Preheat the oven to 350 degrees. Fill crêpes with the cauliflower mixture and line them up in a baking dish. Cover them with the tomato sauce and sprinkle with cheese. Bake until bubbling hot, about 30 minutes.

SERVES 4–6

Tofu Lasagna with Mushrooms, Goat Cheese, and Chard

This version of lasagna uses only one sauce and requires you to do very little ahead of time. It is fun to cook and is a great way to serve fresh pasta. Don't be limited to these particular fillings—serve what is freshest and most beautiful. Add roasted eggplant and squash at the height of summer. And of course, adding a rich Béchamel Sauce (see page 214) to anything will make it extra special.

1 pound dried pasta or 1½ pounds Fresh Pasta (see page 148)

SAUCE

1½ cups chopped onions

½ cup diced carrots

½ cup diced celery

4 to 6 garlic cloves, minced

1 tablespoon dried Italian herb seasoning

1 cup red wine

2 cups crumbled tofu

4 to 5 cups diced tomatoes (canned or fresh)

FILLING

1 bunch chard (spinach or kale also works well)

1 pound mushrooms, washed and quartered

About 1 pound goat cheese, softened

1 egg

1¼ cups grated Parmesan cheese, divided

Salt and pepper

3 cups grated provolone, mozzarella, fontina, or Gruyère cheese

To make the sauce, sauté the onions, carrots, and celery over medium-high heat until softened and beginning to brown. (Make sure the pan you use is big enough for the tomatoes and tofu too.) Add the garlic and herb seasoning to the pan, but do not stir. Turn up the heat and let the onions, carrots, and celery brown, then add the wine to the pan and scrape up all those caramelized bits that bring a lot of flavor to the dish. Add the tofu and cook, stirring frequently, until most of the liquid in the pan is gone. (Sometimes tofu will be particularly watery. It's OK to drain some of the liquid if you are in a hurry.) You want the tofu to brown a little and pick up all the flavors from the pan before you add the tomatoes. When the tofu is ready, add the tomatoes and simmer for 30 minutes or more.

To make the filling, wash the greens, remove the stems, and set stems aside. Sometimes I cook them with the onions in the sauce but usually I just chop them into bite-size pieces and blanch.

Blanch the greens in a pot of boiling water or steam them until just cooked through. Submerge in a bowl of cold water to keep them brilliantly green. Drain the greens in a colander. When they are cool enough to handle, chop roughly. Roll them up in a clean lint-free towel and squeeze out as much liquid as possible; set aside until assembly.

Bake the mushrooms on a baking sheet in a 425-degree oven or sear them in batches in a skillet on the stovetop. When they are done, put them aside with the greens. If your bowl is big enough, you can mix them all together to streamline the assembly process.

In a separate bowl, mix together the goat cheese, egg, Parmesan cheese, and about ½ teaspoon salt. Now you have sauce on the stove and 2 or 3 bowls of prepared fillings as well as 3 cups of some meltable cheese.

If you are using dried lasagna sheets, parboil the pasta so that it is softened but not completely al dente. Fresh pasta does not need to be cooked, but some recipes have you boil the sheets for just 1 minute. This sort of seals the starches and sets the proteins a bit so that the pasta will not soak up as much of the sauce.

Oil a 9 x 13-inch baking dish. Ladle a little sauce into the dish and then cover with a sheet of pasta. Spread one-fourth of the filling ingredients evenly over the pasta and cover with sauce. (Spread out some goat cheese, then some greens and mushrooms, and cover with mozzarella or whatever you choose.) Put down another sheet of pasta and repeat layers three more times. Make sure there's lots of tofu in each layer! Finish with a layer of pasta and more sauce. Top with a sprinkling of Parmesan or—for an extravagant extra layer—a few cups of Béchamel Sauce. Bake at 350 degrees for about 30 to 45 minutes until the sauce is bubbling and the top is browned.

SERVES 6–8

Annie's Frittata with Caramelized Onions, Goat Cheese, and Sage

The flavors of this frittata are wonderfully appealing—the richness of the caramelized onions is just right with the tangy goat cheese and the pungent earthy sage. A glaze of reduced balsamic vinegar is the final touch—brushed over the warm frittata, its sweet acidity highlights the unusual flavors.

2 tablespoons light olive oil, divided
3 large onions, about 2 pounds, quartered
    and thinly sliced
½ teaspoon salt
⅛ teaspoon pepper
3 garlic cloves, finely chopped
8 eggs, beaten

⅓ cup grated Parmesan cheese
1 tablespoon chopped fresh sage
3 ounces mild, creamy goat cheese,
    crumbled
3 tablespoons Reduced Balsamic Vinegar
    (see page 204)

Preheat the oven to 325 degrees.

Heat 1 tablespoon oil in a large skillet; add the onions, salt, and pepper. Sauté over medium heat for about 10 minutes. Add the garlic; continue to cook over medium heat for about 40 minutes, gently scraping the pan with a wooden spoon to keep the onions from sticking as they caramelize. (Add a little water if needed to loosen the sugars from the pan.) Set aside to cool.

Stir together the eggs, onions, Parmesan, and sage. In a 9-inch sauté pan with an ovenproof handle, heat the remaining oil to just below the smoking point. Swirl oil around sides of the pan to coat. Turn heat down to low and immediately pour mixture into the pan. The eggs will sizzle from the heat. Crumble in the goat cheese and cook over low heat for 5 minutes, or until the sides begin to set; transfer to the oven and bake, uncovered, for 20 to 25 minutes, or until golden and firm. Loosen the frittata gently with a rubber spatula (the bottom tends to stick to the pan). Place a plate over the pan, flip it over, and turn out the frittata. Brush the bottom and sides with Reduced Balsamic Vinegar and cut into wedges. Serve warm or at room temperature.

NOTE: *At Tassajara, we always begin cooking our frittatas on the stove, but they can also be cooked entirely in the oven. Combine the cooked vegetables and eggs as directed, but don't add the cheese. Pour mixture into an oiled baking dish, then sprinkle cheese over top. Bake for about 25 minutes.*

SERVES 4–6

Stuffed Peppers with Pine Nuts, Apricots, and Mint

As you cook, taste continually to adjust and balance flavors. Below is a template to get started, but as you become familiar with the process, you may wish to play with it more: use fresh dill, or a pinch of saffron, or substitute almonds for pine nuts, for example. Trust in your senses and allow your intuition to lead the way.

2 cups uncooked short-grain brown rice
Salt
8 bell peppers, any color
2 tablespoons currants
2 tablespoons golden raisins
¼ cup coarsely chopped dried Turkish apricots (unsulfured)
3 tablespoons extra virgin olive oil, plus more for drizzling
1 red onion, chopped
1 tablespoon salt
2 to 3 garlic cloves, minced
2 teaspoons cinnamon, plus more

2 cups diced tomatoes
2 teaspoons honey
⅛ teaspoon cayenne pepper
Zest and juice of 1 lemon
¼ cup pine nuts
3 tablespoons chopped fresh flat-leaf parsley
3 tablespoons chopped fresh mint leaves
3 tablespoons chopped fresh cilantro leaves
⅓ cup crumbled feta
3 cups tomato sauce (optional)

Soak the rice for an hour or longer; drain and rinse. Bring 4 cups cold water to a boil in a pot and then add the rice and a healthy pinch of salt. As soon as the water boils, reduce the heat to low, cover the pot with a tight-fitting lid, and simmer for 50 minutes until cooked.

While the rice is cooking, wash and prepare the peppers: carve out the tops with stems intact and save them to later recap the peppers. Remove the white ribs and seeds within.

In a small bowl, soak the dried fruits in boiled water for 10 minutes to soften them and then drain.

In a skillet, heat the oil and sauté the onion over medium heat until translucent. Add the salt, garlic, and cinnamon. When the mixture becomes aromatic, stir in the tomatoes. Reduce the heat and add the honey, cayenne pepper, and the lemon zest and juice. Remove from the heat and set aside. In a dry skillet, lightly toast the pine nuts until they release their natural oils and begin to turn golden brown. (Pine nuts toast quickly, so watch closely.)

In a large mixing bowl, combine the cooked rice, fruits, tomato mixture, herbs, cheese, and pine nuts; mix thoroughly. Taste for acidity; if needed, add more salt, cinnamon, or cayenne pepper; correct the seasonings, keeping in mind that the flavors will intensify when cooked. If the rice appears dry, stir in some extra olive oil.

Preheat the oven to 375 degrees. Stuff each pepper to the brim with the rice mixture and replace its top. Situate the peppers in a heavy-duty casserole dish suitable for the oven. Drizzle with olive oil. If you choose to use the tomato sauce, pour it over and around the peppers so that they are covered halfway. Otherwise use water in its place to steam the peppers. Cover and cook for 30 to 40 minutes, or until the rice is heated through and the peppers are soft. Do not steam so long that the peppers lose their form.

SERVES 6–8

beans & legumes

Basic Bean Recipe

This is just a basic technique. You can add all sorts of spices and seasonings to beans as they cook, but not acids (like tomatoes) or salts until they're cooked through. These things tighten up the proteins in the skins and make them less open to soaking up water (and heat) into their interiors, so they take much longer to cook.

1 cup beans

Cover beans with at least 3 inches of water and soak overnight or as long as you can. Some people like to start soaking in the morning and have beans for dinner that night. Don't leave beans soaking for more than 24 hours though, or they can start fermenting and growing dangerous bacteria. If you need to hold them for another day, change the water and put them in the refrigerator. When ready, drain and rinse the beans in a colander. Put the beans in a large pot with enough water to cover by about 4 inches. Turn the heat up and bring the beans to a boil. Skim off any foam that forms. When the pot begins to bubble, turn the heat down and simmer until done. This will take as little as 30 or 40 minutes for some lentils to as long as a few hours for chickpeas or 8 to 10 hours for some soybeans. The older the bean, the longer it will take to cook. Most beans take about 2 to 3 hours to cook. Test the beans for doneness by mashing one against the roof of your mouth with your tongue. It should mash easily without leaving any granular chalky bits. Season with a little salt, and you are ready to dress up your beans in any way you like.

SERVES 4

Beans

—DALE KENT

Beans are a major staple at Tassajara. As tenzo, I would try to serve them at least every other day. They are an important source of visible protein in a vegetarian diet. Some people have a hard time digesting beans, but my experience is that most people get acclimated to a heavy bean diet after a very short while.

The gassiness that is associated with beans comes from indigestible complex sugars called oligosaccharides, and there are some things that can be done to beans to make them less "gassy." The main thing is to cook beans completely. A cooked bean should be creamy all the way through.

Skimming the surface scum that rises as the beans begin to cook also helps. Sometimes you have to skim four or five times over half an hour or more before the foam subsides. Make sure to keep the lid off the pot and to not let the beans boil too vigorously during this initial period of cooking so that the foam isn't just washed back into the solution. A nice simmer with bubbles that float to the top but do not break too explosively is what you're looking for. You want the layer of scum to form a kind of cohesive mass that you can skim with a small strainer or slotted spoon. Be gentle as you take the foam off; you can usually remove it in one or two swipes. The more you break the surface tension, the more sweeps you'll have to make; and you'll find that a lot of the stuff you want to remove is actually disappearing right into the broth.

Two additions that can be made to any pot of beans to aid digestibility are kombu or epazote. Kombu is a Japanese seaweed that is a base ingredient for most Japanese soup stocks. Minerals in kombu soften bean skins and thus facilitate penetration of water and heat into the center of the beans. Epazote, an herb traditionally used in Mexican cooking, also helps to make beans more digestible. The flavor of epazote is distinctive, but after cooking, it tastes similar to oregano.

Beans should be completely covered by water throughout the cooking process. Put some water on so that if the water over the beans is starting to cook down, you have boiling water to add. Adding hot water keeps their tender skins from getting shocked and splitting or cracking.

White Bean Salad

White Bean Salad

This is a nice way to eat beans in the middle of a hot summer when you are tired of soup. With corn or rice thrown in, you have a quick one-bowl meal.

2 cups navy (white) beans, sorted, washed, and soaked
4 garlic cloves
6 to 8 cups water
Salt and pepper

½ cup Garlic Oil (see page 206)
6 tablespoons balsamic vinegar
¾ cup diced carrots
¾ cup diced celery
3 to 4 tablespoons chopped chives or parsley

Bring the beans to a boil with garlic and water, and cook until done, about 1 to 2 hours depending on the age of the beans. When cooked through, add salt and pepper to taste. Dress them with the Garlic Oil, vinegar, carrots, and celery. The beans should still have enough residual heat to cook the carrots and celery a little. This salad can be served warm or chilled. Serve within 3 to 4 days.

SERVES 6–8

Butch's Black-Eyed Peas

Butch Baluyut, photographer, monk, and loving friend, lived at Tassajara and City Center for many years. His loving spirit is missed, but his black-eyed peas live on.

3 cups chopped onions
2 tablespoons olive oil
1½ tablespoons minced ginger
3 garlic cloves, minced
1 teaspoon oregano

4 cups black-eyed peas, sorted, washed, and soaked
Salt and pepper
1 lemon, juice and zest

Sauté onions in oil until they are a little caramelized. Add ginger, garlic, and oregano and cook briefly—a few minutes will do. Add beans to onions and season with salt and pepper. The longer this all cooks together, the better the soup gets. Add lemon zest and juice just before serving.

SERVES 6–8

Using What's at Hand: A Story of Creation

—GABE FIELDS

The way I remember it, Butch had this huge pot of black-eyed peas on the stove. I'm not really sure what his plan was for them, or if he had any plan at all. In any case, there had been some kind of food prep mistake that day, and there was all this extra chopped garlic, ginger, and lemon juice just sitting in the walk-in—and I do mean a lot. Butch greedily pulled it all out and arrayed it on the counter: mounds of pungent spices and a generous container of fresh lemon juice. You got the feeling that for Butch, it was golden treasure that simply had to be used. I recall a wave of skepticism as Butch dumped the full containers of ginger and garlic into an onion sauté ("with black-eyed peas?" I thought). But it smelled great, and, as serve-up time approached, Butch seemed confident and pleased with his creation. Another wholesome Tassajara lunch. Time for a nap. But no, there was more. The real clincher. The defining gesture. The step off of the 100-foot pole. The container of lemon juice. Not a splash, or a quarter, or even half of it. All of it. I cringed. Butch tasted it, and asked me to try it. My palate lit up and a shadow was cast upon all other black-eyed pea recipes.

Refried Beans

This is one of the best things to do with leftover beans. Unlike traditional recipes that rely on lard or bacon fat for richness, this version is flavored with well-cooked onions, cumin, and roasted garlic.

1 large onion, medium-chopped
Oil
1 teaspoon ground cumin
6 to 8 roasted garlic cloves, mashed

6 cups cooked beans (pinto, black, or
    anasazi all work well)
Cooking liquid from the beans (or water
    or stock)
Salt

In a pot that is large enough to fit the beans, sauté the onion in oil over medium-high heat until soft and beginning to turn quite brown. Add cumin early in the cooking so that it gets a little toasted and aromatic.

While the onions cook, roast the garlic. Put whole unpeeled cloves in a small skillet or cast-iron pan over medium-low heat. Leaving the peels on will protect the flesh of the garlic from scorching. The paper-like peels blacken and burn, which gives nice charcoal flavor without imparting the bitter notes that would come from actually eating charred garlic. Turn the garlic regularly so that it cooks evenly. The peels will begin to blacken and the garlic will be mushy and soft.

Add the garlic to the onions and mash it around with a wooden spoon or a spatula. Add beans a few spoonfuls at a time, mashing between each addition. When all the beans are added, pour in the reserved cooking liquid a little at a time until beans reach the desired consistency. You should make them a little "looser" or runnier than you want them to be when you serve them because they will thicken up as they cool down.

SERVES 6–8

Chickpea Stew with Collard Greens and Indian Spices

This hearty stew can be served over rice for a simple dinner or as part of a more elaborate Indian feast with chutney, naan, raita, and rice pudding.

1 cup dried chickpeas, soaked overnight	1 teaspoon salt
2 tablespoons minced ginger	2 tablespoons minced garlic
1 bay leaf	2 tablespoons minced ginger
1 (2-inch) cinnamon stick	1 tablespoon Garam Masala (see page 205)
6 to 8 cups water	1 large bunch collard greens, chopped
1½ cups chopped onions	1 (14-ounce) can tomatoes, with liquid
4 tablespoons coconut oil	Salt and freshly ground black pepper

Drain the chickpeas and rinse them well. Put in a heavy-bottom saucepan with the ginger, bay leaf, cinnamon, and water. Bring the pot to a boil and lower the heat to maintain a gentle simmer. Cook uncovered for at least 1 hour. Add more boiling water if needed. Sometimes they can take as long as 2 to 3 hours, particularly at a higher elevation, where water boils at a lower temperature. I recommend pressure-cooking chickpeas for about 45 minutes.

While the chickpeas cook, sauté the onions in oil with salt over high heat until they begin to brown. Add garlic, ginger, and Garam Masala, and cook for 1 minute. Add greens and sauté until they have wilted and begun to lose their leathery texture, about 8 minutes. Add a little of the cooking liquid from the chickpeas or enough water to come halfway up the collards. Cover the pan to braise the collards for 5 minutes. Add tomatoes and simmer for 10 minutes. You may let this stew longer, up to 30 minutes or so if the chickpeas are not yet done. When the chickpeas are cooked through, combine them with the stewed greens. Taste for salt and pepper, and serve.

SERVES 4–6

French Lentil Salad

French lentils are smaller than their more common brown, red, or yellow cousins. They are a dark green color, and they hold their shape better when cooked. You can make this salad with any sort of lentils, but the cooking time will be a little different, and they might be a little mushy and lose their shape.

1½ cups French green lentils
6 cups water or stock
3 garlic cloves
2 bay leaves
¾ teaspoon salt
3 tablespoons vinegar (sherry or
 champagne vinegar is nice)

3 teaspoons Dijon mustard
½ cup olive oil
½ cup diced carrots
½ cup diced celery
½ cup diced red onion
Salt and pepper

Cook the lentils in water with the whole garlic cloves, bay leaves, and salt. (Normally you add the salt after beans are cooked, but when cooking lentils, it helps them hold their shape and only lengthens the cooking time negligibly.) Simmer lentils for 25 to 30 minutes, or until they are soft and cooked through.

While the lentils cook, make a simple vinaigrette. In a large bowl, whisk the vinegar and mustard together, and then drizzle in the oil while continuing to whisk. Toss the carrots, celery, and onion in the dressing. When the lentils are cooked, drain them and toss them in the bowl with the vegetables and dressing while still warm. Mix thoroughly and taste for salt and pepper.

SERVES 4–6

Mung Dal with Chopped Greens and Tomato

This is a favorite dal to make and to eat, hands down. It's exactly what you crave in an Indian dish: warm cumin, coriander flavors with a variety of textures, and a bright lemony, tomato finish to complement the earthiness of the lentils. Also, it is so easy to make, especially if you group ingredients in bowls according to when they get added, as with the tomato below.

1 cup split mung dal (can substitute split peas)

1½ cups water

5 tablespoons Ghee (see page 205), or a mixture of vegetable oil and unsalted butter, divided

1 large firm ripe tomato, cut into 8 wedges

1½ teaspoons ground coriander

⅛ teaspoon cayenne or paprika

½ teaspoon turmeric

1 teaspoon salt

1½ teaspoons cumin seeds

¼ teaspoon asafetida powder (optional)

½ pound greens, washed, stemmed, and coarsely chopped (spinach, chard, or kale)

1 teaspoon fresh lemon juice

2 tablespoons minced fresh parsley or cilantro

⅛ teaspoon nutmeg

Sort through the dal and discard any stones or debris. Rinse in water and drain; repeat rinsing and draining until wash water is clear. Put the dal, water, and 1 tablespoon Ghee in a large saucepan over high heat. Bring to a boil, stirring occasionally. Reduce heat to moderately low and cover with a tight-fitting lid. Boil gently for 30 minutes, or until the dal is tender and plump. When finished, each bit of dal should be soft and separate, like rice. Don't cook so long that they break down; remove from the heat and drain.

In a bowl, combine the tomato, coriander, cayenne, turmeric, and salt. Heat the remaining Ghee in a large frying pan over moderately high heat. Add the cumin seeds and fry until browned. Add the asafetida. Add tomatoes and spices and then cover and cook for 3 minutes.

Stir in the greens, cover, and cook for another 5 to 8 minutes (optionally, you could add any other vegetables to the mix at this point). Add the dal, lower the heat slightly, and add the lemon juice. Cook briefly, stirring it all together. Serve garnished with the parsley or cilantro and nutmeg.

SERVES 4–6

Chana Dal with Potatoes

Chana dal is the same bean as a chickpea, just a different variety. These baby chickpeas look a lot like yellow lentils, but they are quite different. They hold their shape when cooked instead of turning into one mushy mass. They also have a very low glycemic index, meaning that they are a great form of protein for diabetics and anybody worried about spikes in their blood sugar levels. Most Indian markets carry them. This recipe makes a loose dal that is just a little thicker than pea soup. Add a few extra tablespoons of chana dal if you want a little heartier dish, but do try it with the traditional amounts first to see how you like it.

6 cups cooked potatoes	¼ teaspoon whole cumin seeds
½ cup chana dal or yellow split peas	½ teaspoon fenugreek seeds
3 cups water or stock*	1 cup chopped onion
1 teaspoon salt	1 tablespoon peeled, grated, or minced
2 small serrano chiles	fresh ginger
¼ cup oil (sunflower, if possible)	⅛ teaspoon pepper
¼ teaspoon black mustard seeds	2 tablespoons lemon juice

The potatoes can be prepared one of two ways: Boil them whole in their skins, let them cool, remove the skins, and medium chop; or peel and medium chop, toss with olive oil, sprinkle with salt, and roast at 375 degrees until golden brown, about 30 minutes.

Bring the dal to a boil in the water with ½ teaspoon salt. Cover, lower heat, and simmer for 1 hour for dal or 30 to 45 minutes for split peas; drain, reserve liquid, and set dal aside.

Wash the chiles. Stem and halve lengthwise, scrape out seeds, then halve again lengthwise. (Can also just slice or chop the chiles.) Heat the oil over medium heat. Stir in the mustard, cumin, and fenugreek seeds. In a few seconds, as soon as the cumin and fenugreek seeds darken and the mustard seeds begin to pop, add the chiles. Turn them over once (within a few seconds) and then add the onion and ginger. Stir-fry the onion until translucent or even slightly caramelized. Add the dal, potatoes, remaining salt, pepper, and lemon juice. Mix well and cook over medium heat, stirring frequently but gently, until flavors are mingled. Add some reserved stock as mixture dries or starts to stick.

*Add cinnamon sticks and coriander seeds to the vegetable stock for extra flavor.

SERVES 4

Summer Fukaten—Tassajara Kitchen Manager

—WENDY LEWIS

Five of the six summers I lived at Tassajara, I worked in the kitchen as a guest cook, afternoon and day-off fukaten, two summers as fukaten, and one as tenzo. Based on many conversations I have had, I am one of the only, or one of a very few people, who loved being fukaten in the summer at Tassajara and preferred it over other positions. I saw it as a complex puzzle: how do you get gallons upon gallons of prep done and facilitate the serving each day of six meals while supporting a crew of varied experience, interest, and ability, and make sure that everyone is taken care of in the best possible way? Well, impossible, and yet we do it at Tassajara in the summer, day after day. I was fascinated and intrigued. I saw the necessity of a certain degree of anxiety and pressure, so I decided not to mind it but rather to use it to maintain the energy needed for this daily feat, while balancing that with my appreciation for people, Tassajara and its history, and my own joy in being in that place at that time.

I grew up in cities in borderline poverty and had spent fifteen years of my life working full-time. We never had butter or olive oil or the ordinary "special" ingredients available in the Tassajara kitchen in my home when I was growing up, and I learned to use them and watch them being used every day. Living at Tassajara, I often felt I was in a dream of beauty and plenty. I enjoyed the physicality of the kitchen.

My attitude did not mean that difficulties were ignored or avoided, and I am sure there were people working in the kitchen who were critical of me, my methods, and my intentions—why should Tassajara be any different from the rest of the world? But we also had fun together and that was lovely. And I had opportunities to stretch myself occasionally to bake a cake for the residents or to cook or help someone else cook a special meal for the residents, while accommodating the cooks who were preparing meals for the guests—it was a choreography of time, ovens, burners, and counter space. And, I have to say it, of love. Not so much a love of food or cooking, but of how things happen, how food and cooking come out of all the busyness, effort, bickering, exhaustion, and so on. Love is part of what everyone is doing in the kitchen, but the purview of the fukaten was particularly moving for me.

tofu

Dragon's Head Tofu

There is quite a collection of cookbooks in the Tassajara kitchen, and this recipe is in a now out-of-print cookbook titled Food in a Japanese Mood *(1984), by Yukiko Haydock and Robert Haydock. This was one of those cases where scaling-up the recipe to serve 250 people worked, and it was served many times throughout the guest season.*

Vegetable oil
1 block firm tofu, pressed to remove water
4 medium fresh shiitake mushrooms
    (or reconstituted dried shiitake
    mushrooms), julienned
2 tablespoons toasted sesame oil
2 garlic cloves, crushed

½ teaspoon sea salt
1 tablespoon mirin or white wine
1 egg, whisked
½ cup julienned carrots
¼ cup cooked peas
2 tablespoons thinly sliced scallions

Heat enough oil to 350 degrees in a pan large enough to submerge a golf-ball-size dragon head. Crumble tofu into a large bowl. Sauté mushrooms with sesame oil, garlic, salt, and mirin until tender and flavorful; add to tofu mixture and let cool. Mix in the egg, carrots, peas, and scallions. Gently form balls and drop into heated oil. Cook until brown, then place on a cooling rack to drain. Serve warm or at room temperature on a bed of sprouts or Napa cabbage with your favorite sweet or savory Asian sauce.

SERVES 4–6

Sweet Ginger Tofu

This is a great tofu recipe—simple and delicious!

1 pound firm tofu	¼ cup dark sesame oil
½ cup soy sauce	½ ounce dry shiitake mushrooms
¾ cup water	1½ teaspoons dry mustard
½ cup mirin	2 tablespoons minced ginger
⅓ cup sugar	2 tablespoons minced garlic

Slice tofu into ½-inch-thick slices and then layer in a pan so that it has the maximum surface exposed. Combine remaining ingredients and bring to a boil. Simmer for 10 minutes or longer. Pour hot marinade over tofu and let sit. Refrigerate for days, or until dinner.

NOTE: *If in a hurry, bake tofu in the marinade for 30 minutes in a 350-degree oven, then drain it and continue cooking on a sheet tray until done. The flavor will intensify as the water cooks out. Coat the pans with a little extra oil and turn the oven up to 425 degrees if you want to crisp it up a bit.*

Tempeh and Potatoes in Thai Green Curry

Tempeh is a fermented soy food originally from Indonesia and has a great nutty flavor and chewy texture when handled properly. The secret to cooking tempeh is to make sure it is cooked thoroughly, which usually means steaming or cooking it in a broth for 20 minutes before adding it to your dish.

1 package tempeh, cut into small cubes	1 tablespoon brown sugar
1 (14-ounce) can coconut milk	2 tablespoons soy sauce
½ cup water	2 cups peeled and cubed red potatoes
1 to 2 tablespoons prepared Thai green curry paste	Whole cilantro leaves

Steam the tempeh for 20 minutes.

In a wide saucepan, add the coconut milk, water, curry paste, brown sugar, and soy sauce. Add the tempeh and potatoes; simmer for 20 to 25 minutes, or until the potatoes are tender. Garnish with cilantro leaves.

SERVES 4–6

Ma Po Tofu

This recipe is incredibly fast to prepare, delicious, and very flexible. Adding the optional ingredients can be almost as fast if you remember to start the dried ingredients soaking half an hour before you begin prepping the ingredients. This is a vegetarian adaptation of the popular Szechuan dish. Actually, this recipe is all about adapting; one of the first things that a guest cook learns is that it's par for the course to adapt to changing circumstances!

3 tablespoons peanut oil

4 scallions, chopped in small coins, whites and greens separated

1 tablespoon finely chopped ginger

1 tablespoon minced garlic

Small handful dry cloud ears (a Chinese fungus; can also use wood ears), soaked in hot water 20 minutes, rinsed, finely chopped, and any hard roots discarded (optional)

Small handful dry shiitake mushrooms, soaked in hot water 30 minutes, finely chopped, any hard stems discarded

1 teaspoon salted preserved black beans (optional)

3 blocks soft tofu, drained and chopped into ¾-inch cubes (can substitute silken tofu—just be very delicate in handling as it easily dissolves into mush)

1 tablespoon chili bean paste (can substitute other Asian chili sauces like Sriracha)

1½ tablespoons rice wine or dry sherry

1 tablespoon light soy sauce (not low sodium—can substitute tamari)

2 teaspoons sugar

3 cups vegetable stock

1 teaspoon cornstarch mixed with 1 tablespoon water

Ground Szechuan pepper

Heat a wok or cast-iron pan over high heat and add the oil. When oil starts to smoke, add the scallion whites, ginger, garlic, cloud ears, and mushrooms. Stir-fry about 1 minute, then add black beans, crushing them in the pan and blending well. Add everything else except the cornstarch mixture, pepper, and scallion greens. Cook 3 to 4 minutes, stirring occasionally and gently so as not to mash the tofu. Add cornstarch mixture to thicken; garnish with the pepper and scallion greens.

SERVES 8–10

Mu Shu Tofu

This is a vegetarian dish that satisfies even the most die-hard meat eaters.

1 pound tofu, mashed and broken up
Corn oil
3 to 4 tablespoons minced garlic
3 to 4 tablespoons rice wine or dry sherry
2 to 3 tablespoons soy sauce
1 teaspoon sugar
1 to 2 tablespoons Szechuan pepper/salt
    blend*
2½ cups onions (1⁄16-inch quarter moons)
1½ cups crimini or button mushrooms,
    thinly sliced
2 cups shredded cabbage

1½ cups grated or matchstick carrots
1 cup thinly sliced bamboo shoots
4 shiitake mushrooms, simmered,
    stemmed, finely sliced (save liquid for
    another use)
1 ounce black fungus or cloud ear, soaked,
    drained, rinsed well, and chopped into
    shreds
Salt and pepper
Plum or hoisin sauce
Green onion shreds
12 thin flour tortillas

Heat tofu in corn oil over low heat for 20 to 30 minutes, or until it begins to dry out. Add garlic and stir to cook. Add wine and let it boil away. Add soy sauce, sugar, and half of the Szechuan blend; cook until tofu is pretty dry. Taste and add more Szechuan blend. It should be strongly flavored, as it is meant to flavor the entire dish. Set this aside to marinate while you prep the vegetables.

Over high heat, stir-fry the onions until translucent. Add the crimini mushrooms and cook for a few minutes more so that the mushrooms release their juices and start to brown. Add the cabbage and carrots, and cook for a few minutes until the cabbage is wilted. Add the bamboo shoots, shiitake mushrooms, and black fungus. Mix in the tofu just to get it hot and then taste for salt and pepper. Serve with plum sauce, green onion shreds, and steamed tortillas.

Made by toasting a blend of two parts Szechuan peppercorns and one part salt in a dry skillet until aromatic and just starting to smoke. Grind by hand with a mortar and pestle.

SERVES 6–8

Corn Oil

—MEG LEVIE

In April, before the guest season started, the guest cooks were creating practice meals for the community, and Jeffrey Schneider had come down from City Center to help train us. I was the guest cook making breakfast that morning, and Brooks Prouty was assisting me. We were putting on a pretty big production, trying out breakfast burritos. I imagined warm tortillas, scrambled tofu, grated Monterey Jack cheese, avocado slices, and two different salsas: a fresh tomato pico de gallo and a green salsa with serrano chiles.

I was cooking the tofu in the big wok, and it was almost time for breakfast. We were worried about time and were moving fast—steaming the tortillas, getting the serving dishes out, slicing the avocado. The tofu was starting to stick to the bottom of the wok, so I reached for the glass jug of corn oil that was kept under the counter and saw that it was empty. When I had come in earlier I had noticed, with some annoyance, that the large plastic jug of extra corn oil had been left out on the small back counter near the sink. In the midst of the activity I strode over, grabbed the big jug of what I thought was yellow corn oil and poured a dollop on the tofu in the wok, set the jug down on the counter behind me and stirred it all up. When I turned back around to go on to the next thing, my eyes caught the words written on the jug: DISH SOAP. I stopped.

For one awful, tantalizing moment I thought, "What if I don't say anything?" But the vision of what exactly that would mean for the gastrointestinal comfort of the community was too much to bear. I set down the spatula and just stood there, watching with an odd sense of detachment as Jeffrey and Brooks continued the whirlwind of checking the tortillas, pouring the salsa, and glancing at the clock. Finally they noticed that I was still just standing there with an odd expression on my face.

"What?" Brooks asked. I looked at the big plastic container sitting on the counter and they followed my gaze.

"Dish soap," I said quietly. "I thought it was corn oil." Pause. "It's in the tofu."

They looked at me. They looked at the container. They looked at the tofu. They looked at me again. "Oh," they said. "Oh."

Breakfast that morning was granola with tortillas and salsa on the side.

Mole Verde with Tofu

This is a wonderful recipe. It does require a little advance planning. You can marinate tofu for at least one day but preferably three.

TOFU MARINADE

6 tablespoons sherry

2 tablespoons sherry vinegar

1 cup water

6 garlic cloves, minced

¼ teaspoon toasted and ground
    coriander seeds

4 black peppercorns

2 tablespoons corn oil

¼ cup chopped white onion

1 bay leaf

1½ teaspoons salt

3 cups tofu, cut into large chunks

SAUCE

1½ cups roughly chopped, husked, and
    washed tomatillos

1 small onion, cut into thin strips

1 to 2 jalapeños, seeded and minced

8 leaves romaine lettuce, roughly chopped

2 tablespoons minced garlic

1 bunch cilantro, large stems removed

1 to 2 cups stock or water

1 cup pumpkin seeds, toasted until they
    start to pop (can be done in a 350-degree
    oven or in a skillet on the stove)

½ teaspoon ground cumin seeds

3 peppercorns, ground

3 whole cloves, ground

3 allspice berries, ground (optional)

½ teaspoon ground cinnamon

3 tablespoons corn oil

Simmer all the marinade ingredients except the tofu in a small pan for about 20 minutes and then strain. Put the tofu in a bowl and cover the with marinade. Add water or more sherry if you need to completely cover. Refrigerate overnight or up to three days. Stir regularly—at least once or twice a day so that all the surfaces of the tofu get nice exposure.

To make the sauce, simmer the tomatillos, onion, jalapeños, lettuce, garlic, and cilantro in stock or water to barely cover until tomatillos soften and turn yellowish. Blend with a stick blender or transfer to a standing blender. (Be careful not to add too much stock. You want this to be a little thick because if there's too much liquid now, the final sauce will take a long time to thicken up.)

Meanwhile, grind the pumpkin seeds. Traditionally this would be done on a metate or large grinding rock, but at Tassajara we use a hand-cranked seed grinder. A food processor works well too.

In a bowl, mix the ground pumpkin seeds, cumin, peppercorns, cloves, allspice, and cinnamon together. Add just enough stock to make a purée, maybe 3 to 6 tablespoons. Sauté this mixture in a deep-sided pan with the oil for 5 to 10 minutes, or until it thickens and darkens. Stir constantly to keep it from sticking and add more oil if needed. Add the tomatillo purée and cook until thick. Then add stock until it is about the consistency of gravy. Simmer 30 minutes; season with salt.

While the sauce simmers, drain tofu. Roast on lightly oiled baking sheets in a 450-degree oven until there is a little crust, or fry it in oil. If you have the time and the patience, flip the pieces of tofu so that they are crisp all over. Let them cook long enough on each side so that the tofu releases easily from the pan. (There's a stage where it looks and smells as if you should flip them, but you'll only tear off the skin that's forming if you force them to move when they don't want to let go.) When the sauce is done, add tofu and simmer briefly to meld flavors.

SERVES 6–8

Stay in Your Body

—KATHY EGAN

One of the things that I learned during my time in the Tassajara kitchen was very simple, but it has been incredibly helpful in my life.

I was at the stove, singing, stirring a pot, my mind a million miles away. My tenzo came up behind me and gently put her hand and my shoulder and said, "Stay in your body, Kathy."

Basic Tofu Sausage

This is a very basic recipe that can be a springboard for your imagination. Try this with sage, fennel, and Italian herbs for pizza topping or lasagna filling, or as an addition to your favorite spaghetti sauce. Or make it with chile powder, coriander, and lots of cumin for taco filling or a nacho topping.

½ cup minced onion

2 to 4 garlic cloves, minced

2 to 3 teaspoons dried Italian herbs

2 to 3 tablespoons olive oil

1 (14-ounce) block tofu, crumbled

Salt and pepper

Sauté the onion and garlic with the herb seasoning in the oil. Make sure there is a generous coat of oil in the bottom of the pan and add the tofu, salt, and pepper. Continue to cook over high heat, stirring regularly to prevent serious sticking. The tofu will release some water. Continue cooking until the liquid has boiled off. You can now serve this for breakfast or continue cooking so that you start to get some nice fried flavor. Don't be afraid to add a little more oil. It's also nice to take the crumbled tofu and onion, and bake it at 425 degrees on an oiled pan for about 20 to 25 minutes. This dries out the tofu and concentrates the flavors, making it very sausage-like.

NOTE: *If you marinate the tofu in a little dressing of soy sauce, oil, sugar or honey, and black pepper before baking it, you can make your own "bacon bits" for salads or soup condiments. Marinate it right in the cooking dish. Let sit for 30 minutes, then drain and bake the tofu on sheet pans in the oven.*

SERVES 4–6

Tofu Neatballs

This recipe can be made into patties and fried on a griddle for a tasty tofu burger, but they really come into their own served with Simple Tomato Sauce (see page 209) and pasta.

20 ounces tofu
3 to 4 tablespoons olive oil
1 small onion, minced
¼ teaspoon ground cumin
1 teaspoon dried sage
½ teaspoon dried oregano
½ teaspoon dried thyme
2 garlic cloves, minced
½ teaspoon fennel seeds, crushed
½ teaspoon ground allspice

⅓ teaspoon freshly ground black pepper
Pinch cayenne pepper
½ teaspoon dry mustard
2 to 3 tablespoons peanut butter
⅓ cup breadcrumbs (cracker crumbs
    work well too)
¼ cup minced fresh parsley
1 to 2 teaspoons soy sauce
1 tablespoon flour
Salt and pepper

Crumble tofu with your hands into a large bowl.

Heat a sauté pan over high heat with the oil. Sauté the onion with the cumin, sage, oregano, and thyme until the onion is translucent and begins to brown, about 7 to 10 minutes. Add garlic and cook 1 minute. Turn off the heat and stir in the fennel, allspice, black pepper, cayenne, and dry mustard to combine. Stir in 2 tablespoons peanut butter. Combine this mixture with the tofu, breadcrumbs, parsley, soy sauce, flour, salt, and pepper. Mix together well and taste to check for spices and salt. Test the consistency to see that you can make 1- to 2-inch balls that stay together. The neatballs are fragile but should be sticky enough to hold together. If not, add a little more peanut butter and a little flour to help bind them together.

Bake on a sheet pan in a 350-degree oven until brown, about 30 to 40 minutes. Or you can brown them on all sides in a pan on the stovetop. If they break apart while cooking, don't worry—you can just call it tofu sausage or add some canned diced tomatoes for an easy sauce.

SERVES 6–8

Tofu Ragout

Burning off the alcohol content before cooking the wine is an optional step.

1 bottle red wine (750 mL)
3 cups Mushroom Stock (see page 200)
2 cups water
1 to 2 bay leaves
6 tablespoons sweet butter, divided
1 tablespoon corn oil (or coconut or peanut oil)
18 to 24 pearl onions, peeled and cut at the root end
6 cups button mushrooms, briefly washed and dried

1 cup chopped onion
1 cup diced carrots
2 garlic cloves, minced
1 teaspoon dried thyme
4 tablespoons flour
2 tablespoons nutritional yeast (optional)
1 to 2 tablespoons tomato paste
2½ cups cubed tofu (cut into 1-inch cubes)
Salt and pepper

Put wine into a stockpot and bring to a boil. Light it with a match to burn off the alcohol. When flame subsides, add mushroom stock, water, and bay leaves. Bring to a boil, and then simmer uncovered for 45 minutes; strain and measure. If it has not reduced to 4 cups of liquid after straining, boil it down. If it is less than 4 cups, add water.

In a frying pan large enough to hold the onions in one layer, brown 2 tablespoons butter until light brown; add corn oil. Sauté the onions until browned over most of the surface, then add ¼ to ½ cup stock. Cover and cook on the stovetop or in a 350-degree oven until tender.

Just barely glaze in a wok or other open pan with corn oil and heat until almost smoking. Add the mushrooms and stir-fry over high heat until cooked. It's fine if they give up some liquid toward the end; just add it to the stew.

Brown remaining butter then sauté the onion and the carrots until the onion is soft and browned a bit here and there. Add garlic and thyme and sauté until fragrant. Add flour and nutritional yeast (if using) and fry for 2 to 3 minutes. Add tomato paste. Add stock a little at a time then faster as the sauce becomes more liquid. Bring to a simmer and then add tofu, onions, and mushrooms. Simmer for 5 to 10 minutes to meld flavors. Salt and pepper to taste. Serve with boiled potatoes or noodles sprinkled with a little bit of parsley.

SERVES 6–8

"In our everyday life you always have a chance to have enlightenment. Whatever you do. If you go to the restroom there is a chance to attain enlightenment. If you cook there is enlightenment."

—SUZUKI ROSHI

grains & pastas

Brown Rice

Brown rice is really best when cooked in a pressure cooker. It only takes 25 to 30 minutes to cook (after you reach full pressure), and each grain has a softer, more gelatinous texture.

2 cups uncooked short-grain brown rice
4 cups cold water

1 teaspoon oil
¼ teaspoon salt

Wash rice in several bowls full of cold water. Be careful not to lose even one grain of rice. Put rice in a heavy-bottom pot with a tight-fitting lid. Cover with 4 cups water and let soak for at least 1 hour and up to 8 hours. Add the oil and the salt, put the lid on, and bring the pot to a boil over high heat. Listen for the sound of the boil rather than lifting the lid to look. When it boils, turn the heat down to low and cook for 1 hour. The water should be completely absorbed, and the rice should be tender and moist. Turn off the heat and let the rice sit, covered, for 5 minutes. With a large, damp wooden spoon or rice paddle, stir the rice from the top down to the bottom. Cover and let it sit for 5 minutes.

SERVES 4

White Rice

Rice is tricky. Each time, it is just slightly different. It depends on the humidity, the pan, the altitude, and the vagaries of the oven gods. The experienced cook hears the rumble of the boil and can see at a glance with one quick stir that the pot should cook on high without a lid for 45 seconds before putting it on low heat, or knows to add a few splashes of hot water at the end before letting it steam for 10 minutes more. Be attentive—with time you will learn what the rice needs.

2½ cups uncooked short-grain white rice   3 cups cold water

Wash rice in several changes of water and let it drain in a colander, sieve, or cheesecloth for 30 minutes. Put rice in a heavy pot with a good tight-fitting lid. Cover with the water and bring quickly to a boil. Turn heat to low and cook for 15 minutes. Turn heat to high for 20 seconds and then turn off heat. Allow to stand for 10 minutes before lifting the lid. Fluff with chopsticks or a fork. If the rice seems too wet, put it back on the heat briefly without the lid.

SERVES 4–6

Jasmine Rice

Some of the earliest cultivation of rice began in central Thailand. Today jasmine rice is one of Thailand's major exports. You can substitute long-grain basmati rice, but the fragrance and flavor will be lacking. Traditionally, Thai cooks do not salt their rice because so many of the sauces that are served are salty enough on their own. But adding a little salt brings out the flavor of the rice.

2 cups jasmine rice   Salt
2¾ cups water

Put the rice and water into a heavy-bottom saucepan with a tight-fitting lid. Let soak for at least 30 minutes but no more than 1 hour. Add a pinch or two of salt, cover the pot, and bring the rice to a boil over high heat. When it reaches a boil, reduce the heat to low and simmer covered for 15 to 20 minutes, or until the water is absorbed. Let sit for 10 to 15 minutes with the lid on. Fluff with a fork and serve.

SERVES 6–8

Washing Rice

—EIHEI DOGEN

To wash the rice properly, carefully watch with clear eyes that not one grain is wasted; then put it in a pot, light the fire, and steam the rice. An ancient said, "When steaming rice, regard the pot as your own head; when washing rice, know that the water is your own life."

Fried Brown Rice

This recipe transforms leftover brown rice into a side dish you would be proud to serve anyone. Add any cooked vegetables you have and maybe an egg or some leftover beans, and you have a wonderful one-bowl meal.

3 to 4 tablespoons olive oil or butter
1 small onion, medium chopped
½ teaspoon salt
1 small carrot, diced
1 stalk celery, diced

1 teaspoon herbes de Provence
2 cups cooked brown rice, crumbled or broken up
1 to 2 cups leftover vegetables, beans, etc. (optional)

Heat a skillet over medium-high heat and add the oil or butter. Sauté the onion, salt, carrot, and celery with herbs until well browned, about 10 to 15 minutes. Add a little more oil if the pan seems dry. Add the rice and stir-fry for about 5 minutes until it is hot and well combined with the vegetables. The rice is now ready to be served, but if you have some time before your meal, turn the heat to low, add a little more oil to the pan, and let the rice sit undisturbed for about 7 to 10 minutes until browned. If it begins to stick, scrape it up, stir the tasty brown bits in, and continue browning with a little more oil. The more time and energy you spend at this stage, the tastier the rice will be. If using leftovers, add them just before serving and cook to heat thoroughly.

SERVES 4

Spanish Rice

Some folks call this "Mexican Rice" or "Arroz a la Mexicana," but there was no rice in the traditional native diet until the Spanish invasion. Sometimes we enrich this delicious rice with vegetables and cooked beans or tofu for a sort of Mexican paella or Aztec jambalaya.

2 tablespoons olive oil

2 cups uncooked rice (white or brown basmati), washed and drained in a strainer

1½ cups stock or water

1 pound tomatoes, chopped, or 1 (14-ounce) can chopped tomatoes, undrained

2 jalapeños, diced

3 tablespoons minced garlic

¾ cup diced onion

1 to 2 teaspoons salt

½ cup peas (optional)

½ cup chopped carrots (optional)

1 bunch cilantro, roughly chopped (optional)

Heat oil over medium-high heat and add rice. It should sizzle if the heat is high enough. Fry the rice for about 10 minutes. It will start to turn golden brown, and the grains of rice will start to sound a little sharper or more crisp as they rub against each other while you stir. This step adds flavor and helps the individual grains of rice maintain their individuality while cooking.

Heat the stock or water in a separate pot. Add the tomatoes, jalapeños, garlic, and onion to the rice, and continue to cook for about 5 minutes. Traditionally, the tomatoes would be roasted and peeled, and then processed with the rest of the vegetables in a mortar and pestle to make a salsa. You can purée them in a blender or food processor if you like, but they're fine a little chunky. Stir frequently and scrape the bottom of the pan so that nothing sticks.

Add the boiling water or stock, salt, the optional peas and carrots, and stir well. Bring to a boil, stir once, and cover the rice. Cook over low heat for about 15 minutes, a little longer for brown basmati. Taste a piece of rice. It should be almost cooked with only the slightest chalkiness in the very center of the kernel. If it is not done, let it cook 5 minutes more and taste again. Turn the heat off and let the rice sit tightly covered for 10 minutes to finish cooking. Garnish with cilantro and serve.

SERVES 6–8

Saffron Rice

Saffron is one of the most expensive spices per pound. It is a very special addition to almost any dish, but it is especially nice with rice. Use as large a pinch of saffron as you can afford and be careful not to let it blacken when you toast it in a dry skillet.

3 cups long-grain rice
Pinch saffron, lightly toasted and
   crumbled
¼ cup warm milk
¼ cup vegetable oil or Ghee (see page 205)

12 cardamom pods
1 (3-inch) cinnamon stick
1 teaspoon salt
6 cups cold water

Rinse the rice until the water runs clear and then soak for 30 minutes; drain in a colander for at least 30 minutes. You can do this as early in the day as you want to.

Soak saffron in the warm milk. In a heavy pot with a tight-fitting lid, heat the oil. (Save the lid for later!) Add the cardamom and cinnamon, and stir a few times to infuse flavor into the oil. Add rice and salt and sauté until translucent, about 7 to 9 minutes for a larger amount, or 3 to 4 minutes for a smaller amount. Pour in the cold water and bring the covered pot to a boil. The less you take off the lid, the more foolproof the recipe will be. You can usually hear when the pot starts to boil. Listen for it instead of using your eyes. Turn the heat off and let the pot stand for 5 minutes. Turn the heat back on high and bring the pot to a boil again. Turn the heat down to low and cook 10 minutes. Let stand another 5 minutes. Now you can finally open the pot. Taste rice to make sure there is no granular chalkiness at the center of the grain. If it's not quite done, cook on low for a few minutes more. Pour the saffron and milk over the rice and fluff quickly with a long fork. Cover and let steam for 5 minutes.

SERVES 6–8

A Way of Life

—JIRYU MARK RUTSCHMAN-BYLER

There is a good Zen tradition of rotating jobs, of having students try out things that don't come naturally to them. When carpenters come to Tassajara, we say, we put them in the kitchen. When chefs come, we put them in the shop.

So when Jerome arrived, a passionate French chef with a dozen years experience at one of the world's top restaurants, it was a surprise that he was immediately assigned to the kitchen. We all learned a lot from him, verbal and nonverbal, and he had great patience with those of us for whom cooking did in fact not come naturally. Occasionally, though, people's ignorance of the essence of cooking became too much for him to bear.

After another one of his exquisite and perfectly executed meals, a guest from the dining room came into the kitchen, where we were scrubbing pots before eating our own dinner. Impressed and genuinely curious, she inquired after the recipe for that night's risotto.

"Risotto!" Jerome cried, indignant, throwing up his hands. "There is no recipe for risotto!" On the verge of exploding, he walked from the dish sink to where the guest stood, rather alarmed, by the kitchen's back door. He paused, and then cried out again, "Risotto!" Turning and walking back to the dish sink, he belted out the rest of his thought: "Risotto . . . is a way of life!"

A way of life, indeed, precisely the Zen way of life, though Jerome wouldn't cheapen either by saying so. Just enough stock, patient, careful stirring; and then a little more stock, more patient, careful stirring . . . timing, rhythm, breath, responsiveness, patience, attention. Just making risotto, just meeting risotto, a way of life that no recipe reaches. That's what Jerome taught us, and what Tassajara, creek and blue jays, garbage pit and zendo, teaches constantly.

Mushroom Squash Risotto

This risotto recipe is different from many in that it doesn't call for cheese. Instead, add several tablespoons of butter just at the end to give body and creaminess.

1 cup crimini mushrooms	6 to 7 cups vegetable stock
3 cups peeled and cubed butternut squash (½-inch cubes)	1 large onion, finely chopped
	2 cups uncooked Arborio rice
½ cup olive oil	1 cup white wine
Salt	4 tablespoons cold butter, cut into chunks
1 tablespoon chopped parsley	Splash of white truffle oil (optional)

Cut mushrooms into quarters (or halves depending on size). Toss the squash with some olive oil and salt. Spread the squash cubes on a baking sheet in a single layer and roast in the oven at 425 degrees until they have begun to brown, about 20 minutes. While the squash is cooking, heat about 4 tablespoons olive oil in a large sauté pan. When very hot but not smoking, add mushrooms and stir. Sprinkle some salt on the mushrooms as they cook and stir periodically so they don't burn. After a while, the mushrooms will absorb the oil, and the pan will appear dry. Keep cooking and stirring, and the mushrooms will release their juices into the pan. Keep cooking until all the water is evaporated and the mushrooms begin to fry in the oil. You can tell when this is happening because the sound will change from bubbling water to sizzling oil. Cook until the mushrooms have begun to brown. Remove from the heat and add parsley; set aside. Bring stock to a slight simmer. Heat some olive oil in a wide sauté pan and add the onion. Cook for a few minutes until the onion is very soft but not brown.

Add the rice and stir well to coat. Keep heat at medium-high and stir for about 2 minutes. Add the wine, which should sizzle violently when it hits the pan (if it doesn't, the heat isn't high enough). When most of the wine has evaporated, start adding the stock a little at a time. The trick to this process is to stir continuously, maintain an active simmer (you should always see bubbles), and add the stock slowly. Add a ladleful at a time and stir until it has become incorporated before adding more. Add salt to taste. When the rice is nearly done (about 15 minutes), add the mushrooms and squash, and keep cooking until rice is completely tender and cooked through. Turn off the heat, add the cold butter, and stir until incorporated. Drizzle with white truffle oil. Taste again for salt and serve.

SERVES 4–6

Sesame Noodles

This hearty noodle salad is even better the next day.

1 pound thin Chinese rice noodles (can substitute vermicelli or other thin Italian pasta)

7 tablespoons light soy sauce (not light or low sodium)

¼ cup dark sesame oil (strong-flavored Asian kind, not the light cooking oil)

3½ tablespoons brown sugar

3 tablespoons black or balsamic vinegar

3 tablespoons water

1 tablespoon grated or minced fresh ginger

2 teaspoons salt

1 teaspoon chili garlic paste (can substitute other Asian chili sauces)

1 to 2 garlic cloves, minced

2 bunches scallions, chopped into thin coins

¼ cup toasted sesame seeds or chopped peanuts

1 pound lightly cooked green beans (can substitute asparagus or broccoli, cut into green-bean-size lengths)

1 red bell pepper, sliced into thin strips (optional)

Slivers of sautéed, grilled, marinated, or baked tofu (optional)

Small handful dry shiitake mushrooms, soaked in water overnight, drained, thinly sliced, any hard stems discarded, saving the soaking water (optional)

Cook the noodles until tender; drain and rinse in cold water to stop the cooking. In a bowl, mix the next nine ingredients together, reserving the cooked vegetables and optional ingredients, and pour over the noodles, tossing well. Add the remaining ingredients and stir together. Serve at room temperature.

SERVES 6–8

Pad Thai

It is surprisingly simple to make really good pad thai. Even without the turnip pickle, this dish tastes very authentic.

2 to 3 garlic cloves, minced

1 to 2 tablespoons coconut oil or other cooking oil

1 cup crumbled tofu, coated with oil and ½ teaspoon salt and fried in a skillet or baked in a hot oven until crisp

2 eggs, beaten

8 ounces dried rice noodles, soaked in hot water for about 20 minutes

2 tablespoons turnip pickle (available in most Asian markets)

4 scallions, cut into long slivers

¼ cup toasted and finely chopped peanuts

1¼ cups bean sprouts

½ teaspoon chili powder, or more to taste

1 teaspoon sugar

4 tablespoons soy sauce

2 tablespoons lemon juice

Cilantro and lemon wedges

Sauté the garlic in oil over high heat for 1 to 2 minutes. Add the fried tofu and stir for 30 seconds. Add eggs and cook until set before stirring them in.

Drain the noodles and add to the pan. Stir well and then add the pickle, scallions, and half of the nuts and sprouts. Stir to combine and then add the chili powder, sugar, and soy sauce. Stir well and add the lemon juice just before serving. Garnish with the remaining nuts and sprouts and a nice bit of chopped cilantro and lemon wedges.

SERVES 4–6

Mint-Cilantro Udon with Fresh Ginger and Meyer Lemon

This is a recipe from Eric Gower's book The Breakaway Japanese Kitchen: Inspired New Tastes *(2003).* *It is a perfect summer meal—light and refreshing.*

1 to 2 tablespoons extra virgin olive oil

2 tablespoons chopped shallots

6 heaping tablespoons plain yogurt

2 cups chopped fresh mint leaves

2 cups chopped fresh cilantro leaves

2 tablespoons diced fresh ginger

Zest of 2 Meyer lemons, minced, 1 pinch reserved

Juice of 2 Meyer lemons

Sea salt

1 pound udon

Set a pot of water to boil for the udon. Heat the oil in a small skillet. Sauté the shallots for a few minutes and then transfer to a blender. Add everything except the udon and reserved zest to the blender and blend. Cook the udon in the boiling water until al dente; drain, return to the pot, and gently mix in the sauce from the blender. Taste for salt, transfer to warm plates, and sprinkle on the reserved zest.

SERVES 4

Orzo, Red Chard, and Feta

Any green can be used for this recipe but the earthy flavor of red chard complements the feta cheese nicely.

4 cups cold water
1 cup dried orzo
1 bunch red chard
Fruity olive oil
2 teaspoons minced garlic

2 tablespoons red cooking wine
2 ounces goat feta cheese
¼ cup tamari or soy sauce
Salt and freshly ground black pepper

Bring cold water to a boil and cook orzo until tender, about 12 minutes. While pasta is cooking, stem chard, wash stems and leaves, and then slice stems and roughly chop leaves. Sauté stems over medium heat in hot olive oil, garlic, and wine until tender but still crunchy. Add the leaves until slightly wilted—this will happen fast. After the orzo is cooked, remove it from the heat, strain it, and immediately add the chard, feta, and tamari. Add salt and pepper to taste.

SERVES 2

Couscous with Pistachios and Raisins

Toasted pistachios and plump raisins are perfect for dressing up this simple but satisfying grain. Traditional couscous recipes are complicated and include the steps of precooking, soaking, steaming, and sprinkling water. This is the quick and easy way.

3 cups water or stock
1 cup couscous
2 tablespoons olive oil
½ teaspoon salt

½ cup pistachios, toasted
½ cup raisins, soaked in warm water and
    drained

Bring water or stock to a boil. Warm a heatproof dish or pan with a tight-fitting lid in the oven. Put the couscous, oil, and salt in the warm dish and mix together. Make sure that each grain gets coated with a little oil. Pour 2 cups of the boiling water or stock over the top and make sure the couscous is settled in an even layer in the pan. Cover and let steam for 7 minutes. Fluff with a fork and sprinkle in the other 1 cup of boiling water. Cover and let stand for 5 minutes. Garnish with pistachios and raisins just before serving.

SERVES 4–6

Orzo, Red Chard, and Feta

The Dinner Bell

—RAMANA LEWIS

A railroad bell tolled across the narrow valley of Tassajara three times a day in the summer to signal that breakfast, lunch, and dinner was ready for the guests. These times were the sweet spots of the day, as the beehive sound of the guests' chatter in the courtyard faded and thickened into the dining room like a foaming reduction sauce. The sound of this bell was dependable, like the rest of the Tassajara schedule. It was woven securely into the fabric of daily life, like the *han* which called us to *zazen*. In four summers I had heard neither the han falter nor the dinner bell hang silent for a guest meal.

I was the cook the summer of 1994 who stilled the dinner bell for twenty long minutes.

Dinner was spinach ricotta ravioli smothered in a creamy garlic-sage sauce. It started well. In the early afternoon, long, wide sheets of ravioli noodles came spilling obediently out of the pasta machine. They gave off a sweet, floury breath and were as soft as baby skin. I laid them like vast, elastic quilts on the lightly floured counter and spooned the spinach ricotta filling, speckled with herbs, into little heaps at 2-inch intervals. I laid a second sheet on top of each one and cut the quilts into little squares with a pastry wheel. Then I dropped them into a big pot of boiling water, scooped them out with a slotted spoon, and set them twelve-by-twelve into casserole dishes.

In mid-afternoon two things happened that made my heart drop into my shoes. First, I paused to look at the clock and see how long each batch of ravioli was taking. It hit me immediately: the ravioli would never be done in time for dinner. Next, I swirled a wooden spoon experimentally in the cream sauce. It behaved like a vat of milk. It would not be thick enough to decant over the ravioli by dinnertime.

I moved faster. I moved as fast as I could, then faster. But, it was not fast enough. The afternoon passed as quickly as the Tassajara creek. One cook then another heard what was happening, banged open the kitchen door, threw on an apron and helped. Our fingers flew—we hastily formed and boiled over 250 little raggedy, cooled, and gummy ravioli as the guests began arriving in the courtyard for dinner, their shoes crunching the gravel.

The ravioli laid in the bottoms of their dry casserole dishes, gasping for cream sauce. I leaned over the sauce on my stepstool, wringing my hands, willing it to thicken. The head server came in at dinnertime, took the situation in with a single glance and just shook his head. I begged for one more minute. One more minute! Just one more!

The kitchen crew carried away the desserts, salads, and side dishes and came back to wait for the ravioli. They formed a sober line from the serve-up counter all the way out the back door and down the steps. They looked at the clock and the unfinished food. The silence of the dinner bell reverberated through me, leaving me breathless. Outside the kitchen, the voices of the guests grew louder.

Teah Strozer strolled in, wearing clean clothes and a *rakasu,* a bib like garment received in an ordination ceremony that represents Buddha's robe. This was her night to eat with the guests. She didn't say a word. The whole kitchen was in motion. With nothing to do but wait on the sauce, still we were a blur of frantic aprons and hot pads buzzing around each other, checking and rechecking what we already knew.

Teah just stood and looked at me. Seeing her solid, small frame, her calm half-smile, I knew we had to serve the ravioli in unthickened cream. The time was now. I gave the signal and the cooks each took a ladle. We all simultaneously poured out aromatic white baths for each ravioli dish and the servers carried them away. Teah left quictly with them, and her silence spread gently through the kitchen and courtyard. I stood at the counter, my whole body shaking, freely perspiring in the cauldron of the kitchen as the dinner bell tolled.

Fresh Pasta

Pasta is an ingenious food, merely flour and eggs mixed together properly. Dried, it lasts quite a while and is always there in the pantry waiting to provide that comforting sense of "mmmm . . . pasta." Pasta can be somewhat of a guilty pleasure. Whether it is because of the carbs, the wheat, the eggs, or an attempt to eat only whole grains, a lot of people have had to stop eating pasta—and it is often one of the hardest cravings for them to let go of.

2 cups all-purpose flour	3 eggs

Sift flour onto a clean counter. Make a well in the center of the flour and add the eggs. Start stirring the eggs around in the well of flour with a fork. Get the eggs moving in a nice circular pattern as if you were scrambling them for an omelet. Break up the yolks and start pulling in the flour. Continue mixing in the flour from the edge of the well until the dough is too stiff to work with a fork. Start kneading by hand, just as you would for bread.

With clean hands and a scraper on the counter at the ready, pull the farthest edge of the dough towards you and fold the dough in half. Press it down and slightly forward to seal the fold you made and give the dough a quarter turn. Repeat by pulling the farthest edge of the dough towards you and continue kneading until the dough is mixed. You might not have to use all of the flour. If your dough gets a little too dry and crumbly, give it a misting of water from a spray bottle. Let the dough rest at least an hour so that the glutens relax. Just leave it on the counter underneath a damp towel.

You can roll out pasta by hand, but if you have a pasta machine, it is definitely worth using one. Much faster and more fun!

The first step is to complete the kneading process.

1. Press the dough until it is flat and narrow enough to fit through the rollers on the largest setting of your pasta machine.

2. Feed the dough through the top of the machine as you use the crank to compress the dough into an even layer.

3. Fold the dough in on itself and run it through the machine again.

These first runs through the machine complete the kneading process. Now separate the dough into four equal parts. Set aside three pieces and put under a damp towel so they don't dry out.

With your palms, press the dough so that it is thin enough to go through the largest setting of the rollers. Run it through once or twice and then fold the dough in thirds so that you have two sharp, clean edges and a piece of dough that is narrow enough to fit through the machine. Repeat 2 or 3 times.

Get all four pieces of pasta dough to this stage before continuing (otherwise you end up turning the knob on the machine 7 times for each piece of dough—28 times! Not very efficient!). If you thin out all 4 pieces, you need enough clear counter space for the clean towels on which to put the large sheets of pasta you will be systematically working with.

Start running the pasta through the machine and reducing the space between the rollers. Be patient and don't skip too many numbers! Marcella Hazan says that flattening dough "can be compared to reaching the sidewalk from a building's sixth story. The fastest way is to jump, but you will be a mass of shattered bones. One of the reasons that pasta made by shops is generally so mediocre is that the dough is flattened all at one time, rather than step by step: its body is smashed, its vital sinew broken, it is inert." If this doesn't make you want to take your time, I don't know what will.

When the pasta is as thin as you like, you can cut it in the rollers of your machine or cut it by hand. I don't usually mess with cutting the noodles, because when I make fresh pasta, it is almost always for lasagna, which I feel really showcases the texture and flavor of fresh pasta.

To cut noodles by hand, give the pasta a nice sprinkling of flour on both sides. Run your hand across the surface of the pasta to make sure that the dough feels dry and not sticky. Fold the dough so that it is half as long and then fold it in half again in the same direction so that you have a little loose-layered package in front of you from which you can cut long noodles with one quick slice of a chef's knife. A pizza roller works as well. Toss the pasta with a little flour to unfurl the noodles. Fresh pasta cooks in 5 to 6 minutes in a large pot of boiling salted water.

SERVES 4–6

Simple and Delicious Yeasted Tart Dough

This wonderfully rich dough is almost like a brioche dough. It handles very easily, and if all of the ingredients are at room temperature, it comes together very easily. If you forget about getting ingredients out of the fridge hours before you need them, simply put the egg (uncracked) in a bowl of warm water for about 15 to 20 minutes. Cold butter warms up quickly with the heat of your hands, so don't hesitate to get a little messy while you work the eggs into the butter. Sometimes your bare hands are the very best tool in the kitchen, but keep a scraper or spatula nearby so you can clean up quickly. It's amazing how many teaspoons of butter your hands can get coated with. Just don't wash it down the drain!

1 teaspoon dry yeast	½ teaspoon salt
Pinch of sugar	1 large egg
¼ cup warm water	3 tablespoons soft butter
1¼ cups flour, divided	

Dissolve the yeast and sugar in the warm water. Let sit for 10 minutes.

Combine 1 cup flour with the salt in a large bowl. Make a well in the flour and pour in the egg. Make sure the egg is not so cold as to solidify the butter. Add the butter and pour in the yeast mixture. Stir everything together with a wooden spoon. Begin by stirring the liquids together. As they come together, begin picking up more and more flour until you form a smooth dough that pulls away from the bowl. It should come together very quickly. Quick effective strokes that pick up just the right amount of flour are the key.

Turn out the dough onto a counter and knead in the remaining flour until smooth and shiny, about 5 minutes. Put the dough into an oiled bowl and let rise for about 1 hour, or until it has doubled in size. Punch down the dough and let it rise again if you have (or need) the time.

This is a very elastic dough that is really easy to work with. The dough can be hand-worked straight from bowl to pan and simply pressed into a tart form, laid out flat like a pizza with the crust folded up over the filling. Roll out and cajole the dough into a 12- to 14-inch circle to line a 10-inch tart pan. Or pull and fold the dough into a free-form galette baked on a baking sheet.

SERVES 6–8

Pie Crust

2¼ cups all-purpose flour
½ teaspoon salt

1½ sticks cold butter, cut into large pieces
6 to 8 tablespoons ice water

In a bowl, combine the flour and salt. Rub the butter and flour between the palms of your hands, trying to create flat sheets of butter. Work quickly so that the butter does not get too warm. Make a well in the center of the flour mixture and pour the ice water into the center. Cover the water with flour from the sides and let sit undisturbed for 1 minute. Continue to press the flour and water together without stirring the dough. Once it comes together, wrap it in plastic wrap and refrigerate for 30 minutes.

On a floured table, roll the dough out to ½ inch thick. It will still be a little crumbly, so don't worry too much. Fold it in thirds and repeat two more times. By the third time, the texture should be smoother and the dough easier to work with. Wrap again and refrigerate for at least 30 minutes.

Divide the dough in half. On a floured table roll the dough out to the desired shape.

FOR 2 (9-INCH) PIES, 1 DOUBLE-CRUSTED PIE, OR 2 GALETTES

Leave No Trace

—KATHY EGAN

One of the most clear memories of seeing the Zen practice of "leaving no trace" embodied was when Ed Brown came in and made twenty tarts. He didn't pull rank and have others clean up for him. When he left, everything he used was washed and put away, and the baker's counter was cleaner than when he began. In my life after Tassajara, the practice of "leave no trace" has extended beyond my kitchen to all my interactions. I don't want to leave people with a nasty taste in their mouth after an interaction with me. When I leave an encounter, it's so nice to walk away with the feeling of leaving no trace.

Buckwheat Crêpes (Blinis)

These thin pancakes are a great dish to serve to people with wheat allergies. At home we frequently make a batch of these to wrap up our leftovers, but at Tassajara it was a big production to make enough blinis for everyone. Almost anything tastes good against their earthy, toasty, nuttiness, and they are really quite easy. You have to spend half an hour cooking at the stove, but they make even the most humble of leftovers feel like a celebratory feast. Cooking crêpes fills the house with good smells and is a wonderful way of spending time with your family in the kitchen. The pancakes can be prepared a few hours before you need them. Just stack them up and cover them with a damp towel or an upside-down bowl or both to make sure that they do not dry out too much.

1½ cups water	Salt and pepper
3 eggs	Butter
1¼ cups buckwheat flour	

In a large bowl, whisk together the water and eggs. Sift the flour, salt, and pepper into the bowl and stir well; let the batter rest for at least 20 minutes.

Heat the pan over medium-high heat and add a little pat of butter, just enough to coat the pan when it melts. If the pan is the right temperature, the butter should bubble and begin to brown. You only need to add butter to the pan for the first one or perhaps two. If the crepes start to stick or the pan looks a little dry, add another pat of butter.

Pour ¼ cup of the batter in the pan and swirl around so that the batter spreads out into a thin even layer. Cook for about 2 minutes and then flip and cook for about 1 minute more. The crêpe will be flecked with golden brown splotches when they are done. Lightly tap the center of the crêpe. It will spring back when the center is fully cooked.

NOTE: *The simplest, perhaps most classic, thing to do with these crêpes is to fill them with a little meltable cheese. Simply reheat the crêpes over medium-high heat with a little more butter and sprinkle a few tablespoons of grated cheese over top. Fold the crêpe around the cheese into a little square package and serve. I like to serve these with a nice drizzle of roasted red pepper purée.*

NOTE: *If you let the blini batter rest overnight (in the refrigerator, of course), it will be less aerated and not so full of air pockets that expand when the batter hits the pan. This creates holes in the structure of the dough. Pastry chefs tend to make their batter the day before they need it so that the batter pours onto the pan smoothly. Sometimes you can tap the batter bowl on the counter to get some of the bubbles to rise. This sort of works, but you still end up with a little bit of a lacey crêpe. I just pour in a little more batter to cover the holes. They make no difference to the flavor of the final dish.*

Cooking crêpes takes a little practice, but you should get the hang of it after cooking one batch. You don't need a special pan, although a nice, well-seasoned cast-iron pan is nice to use. The first crêpe is always problematic. Eat it yourself or throw it to the chickens, but don't let yourself get disheartened!

SERVES 4–6

A Lover of Pretzels

—GLORIA LEE

The summer baker provides bread for guests and students at lunch every day. This comes to about 60 pounds of dough each day.

Basic bread is water, flour, and yeast with salt added after the first phase. This first phase tests the freshness and potential growth of the yeast. If it proofs well, salt and options such as sweetener and oil are incorporated when adding and kneading in more flour.

On the first lunch of the season, donors were hosted with a picnic. The long thin baguettes I baked for this occasion had risen well and had a crisp crust when they came out of the oven. But, they were almost tasteless. The salt was left out! Later, I found out this happens to almost every baker ONLY once.

As a lover of pretzels, I decided to brush the baguettes with concentrated salt water and a sprinkling of rock salt. A few minutes in the oven dried the salt to the crusts.

A big success and a lifelong lesson to remember the importance of salt in food.

Pizza Dough

Serving pizza is always a festive time at Tassajara for guests and residents alike. The joy and anticipation of these rustic vegetarian pies build as they are carried hot from the ovens across the courtyard to the dining room. Pizza dough is relatively easy to make, and you can store it for a day in the refrigerator or even longer in the freezer, allowing it to thaw for a day in the refrigerator before using it.

1 package (¼-ounce) active dry yeast	3 tablespoons olive oil
½ cup warm water	1¾ cups plus 2 tablespoons warm water
4½ to 5 cups bread flour	(105 to 110 degrees)
2 teaspoons salt	2 to 3 tablespoons fine cornmeal

In a large bowl, add the yeast to the warm water; let sit for 10 minutes until bubbly. Add remaining ingredients. Mix together by hand until a shaggy mass forms. Put dough on a floured counter or board and knead until smooth, about 12 minutes. Add flour as needed, but the dough should be a little sticky. Put into an oiled bowl, turn once to coat. Cover the bowl, place in a warm spot in the kitchen, and let the dough rise until double in size, about 30 minutes. Turn the dough onto the counter. Divide into four even pieces for smaller pizzas or two pieces for larger pizzas. Round each piece into a moderately tight ball. Brush lightly with olive oil, cover, and let rest in the refrigerator for 30 minutes. The dough may also be made a day ahead of time up to this point and refrigerated overnight.

For the final shaping, take a ball of pizza dough and flatten it into a disk. Starting from the middle of the disk, push the dough out evenly with your fingers, working in a circle, until the dough is the desired size, leaving the edges a little thick. Dust a pan with some cornmeal and lay out the pizza dough. Add desired toppings. Bake in a 500-degree oven until the edges are golden brown, about 15 to 20 minutes.

Parmesan Polenta Squares

Soft polenta is a wonderful complement to many vegetarian stews. You can substitute the Parmesan for any number of cheeses. Cheddar, fontina, Gorgonzola, Gouda, or almost any smoked cheese—all work well with this recipe.

6 cups water
1 to 2 teaspoons salt
2 cups coarse cornmeal

1 cup grated Parmesan cheese
1 to 2 tablespoons butter
Olive oil

In a heavy-bottom soup pot, bring water to a boil and add salt. Slowly pour a thin stream of cornmeal into the boiling water while whisking vigorously. (If you pour in too much cornmeal at one time, the individual grains will clump together and form lumps that you can never really break apart.) When all the cornmeal is added, continue whisking for 3 minutes. Turn the heat down to low and cover the pot. Cook about 30 minutes, stirring at least every 5 minutes. If it starts to thicken up so much that it is beginning to be hard to stir, whisk in a little boiling water to thin it out. When the polenta is done, stir in the cheese and the butter.

Pour cooked polenta into a clean baking dish, loaf pan, or a couple of pie pans and smooth the top with a wet spatula to flatten. Cool polenta to let it firm up, at least 20 minutes. Cut into any shape you like. Brush both sides of each piece with olive oil and fry over high heat in an oiled sauté pan until crisp, about 5 to 7 minutes per side. Serve warm.

SERVES 4–6

Naan

Naan is a rich and delicious flatbread from India. It is traditionally cooked on the inside of wall of a tandoor (clay oven). Serve with dal, curry, raita, and apricot chutney for a special meal.

1 package active dry yeast
1 cup warm water, divided
3½ cups bread flour
½ cup whole wheat flour
1 teaspoon salt

3 tablespoons Ghee (see page 205) or
    clarified butter, plus more to brush
    naan when taken out of the oven
1 cup yogurt

In a large bowl, add the yeast to ½ cup warm water; let sit for 10 minutes. Add the flours, salt, Ghee, yogurt, and remaining water. Mix together by hand until a shaggy mass forms.

Put dough on a floured counter or board and knead until smooth, about 12 minutes. Add flour as needed, but the dough should be a little sticky. Put into an oiled bowl and turn once to coat. Cover the bowl, place in a warm spot in the kitchen, and let the dough rise until double in size, about 60 minutes. Turn the dough onto a lightly floured counter. Divide into eight pieces. Round each piece into a ball; cover and let rest 15 minutes.

Flatten each piece into a circle and gently stretch the dough from one side into a rough teardrop shape. Spray with a light mist of water and bake in a 500-degree oven until lightly browned, about 12 to 15 minutes. Brush with Ghee.

SERVES 4–6 ALONE OR 6–8 IF SERVED WITH RICE

Pita Bread

This recipe for pita bread relies on a poolish—a mixture of equal parts flour and water with a tiny amount of yeast added—made the day before the final dough is made. By adding the slowly fermented poolish to the final dough, we can improve the texture and flavor of the bread without a lot of extra work. Making the poolish is fast and can easily be done by hand.

POOLISH

¾ cup warm water

¾ cup bread flour

Pinch of active dry yeast

DOUGH

1 package (¼-ounce) active dry yeast

1½ cups whole wheat flour

1 cup warm water (105 to 110 degrees), divided

1 teaspoon salt

1½ cups bread flour

Poolish (see above)

Make the poolish the day before making the dough; use a container large enough to allow it to double in size. Add the yeast to the warm water and let sit for 10 minutes. Add the flour and mix with your hands or a wooden spoon until all the flour is incorporated. Cover with plastic wrap and leave at room temperature.

For the dough, add yeast to ½ cup of the warm water in a large bowl; let sit for 10 minutes. Add the remaining water and the rest of the ingredients. (Don't forget the poolish!) Mix together by hand until a shaggy mass forms.

Put dough onto a floured counter or board and knead until smooth, about 12 minutes. Put into an oiled bowl, turn once to coat. Cover the bowl with a kitchen towel or plastic wrap, place in a warm spot in the kitchen, and let the dough rise until double in size, approximately 60 minutes. Turn the dough onto a counter. Divide into eight pieces. Round each piece into a ball. Cover and let rest 15 minutes. Roll each piece into a circle about ¼ inch thick, cover, and let proof for 20 minutes. Bake in a 500-degree oven until lightly browned, about 12 to 15 minutes.

SERVES 6–8

desserts

Coffee Flan

The flavor of coffee mixed with the caramel syrup makes this flan a real winner. We use decaf coffee beans at Tassajara, although there was a meal when one of our cooks, a coffee purist, decided to use regular beans. Half of the residents complained the next morning that they had trouble sleeping after eating the flan.

3 cups milk	Lemon juice
1 cup cream	4 eggs
¼ cup coffee beans	2 egg yolks
2 cups sugar, divided	1 tablespoon vanilla
About ⅓ cup of water	

Heat the milk and cream over medium-low heat, stirring constantly. Bring this to a simmer and steep whole coffee beans in milk over low heat for 30 minutes or more. (You can use ground coffee if you like—just reduce the steeping time to 5 minutes and be sure to strain out the grounds!)

To make the caramel, put 1 cup sugar into a small heavy-bottom saucepan. Stir in enough water to make the sugar like wet sand. With a wet finger, brush the side of the pan to remove any remaining sugar crystals. Put the saucepan over medium heat and bring the sugar to a boil. Add a few drops of lemon juice. Once the sugar begins to boil, allow it to cook undisturbed. After a time, the sugar will begin to darken. Swirl the pan gently to distribute the heat. When the color is a light amber, remove the pan from the heat, as the caramel will continue to darken. Pour a thin layer into the bottom of one 4-cup ramekin or 6 smaller ones.

Strain the coffee beans out of the milk and stir in the remaining sugar.

In a large bowl, stir the eggs, yolks, and vanilla together. Slowly whisk the hot milk into the egg mixture. If you pour too fast, you risk cooking the eggs. Once you get about half of the milk into the eggs without scalding them, they are "tempered" and you can add the rest of the milk more quickly. Strain the custard base through a small sieve. Pour the custard base into the prepared ramekins. Bake in a bain-marie (water bath—a deep pan filled with enough water to reach halfway up the side of the custard). This keeps the custard from cooking too quickly. It moderates the heat and keeps the custard from boiling, which creates little bubbles. Bake at 325 degrees until the custard is set, about 25 minutes for small ramekins or 45 to 60 minutes for a large casserole dish.

SERVES 4–6

Torta di Cioccolato e Nocciola
(Chocolate Hazelnut Cake)

This dense, rich chocolate cake really just needs a little dusting of powdered sugar to be perfectly acceptable for the guests, but we often make a chocolate glaze or ganache to spread over the top.

⅓ cup hazelnuts, preferably blanched
Cocoa
¾ cup sugar, divided
½ cup all-purpose flour
4 ounces chocolate, finely chopped
2 tablespoons hot espresso or strong coffee

½ cup butter
3 eggs, separated
¼ teaspoon cream of tartar
Pinch of salt
½ teaspoon Frangelico or Amaretto

Preheat the oven to 325 degrees. Roast the hazelnuts for 8 minutes in the oven. In the meantime, prepare an 8-inch round cake pan by buttering and dusting it with cocoa. After the nuts have cooled, grind them with 2 tablespoons sugar to a fine powder in a food processor.

Sift the flour and combine it with the hazelnuts. If the hazelnuts have skins, rub them in a clean dish-towel until most of the skins are removed.

Melt the chocolate over a double boiler; add the coffee and mix. Keep warm while preparing the other ingredients.

Cream the butter and ½ cup sugar in a mixing bowl until light and fluffy.

Beat the egg whites with the cream of tartar and salt to soft peaks. Add 2 tablespoons sugar and continue beating until stiff peaks form. Beat the egg yolks and Frangelico together, and blend with the warm melted chocolate and coffee. Add one-third of the egg whites to the chocolate mixture to lighten it, and then gently fold in the remaining whites. Sprinkle the flour and hazelnuts into the cake batter while continuing to gently fold all the ingredients together. As soon as the batter is mixed through, pour it into the prepared pan and bake at 325 degrees for about 25 to 30 minutes. The center of the cake should jiggle slightly when done. A toothpick inserted halfway between the center and the edge should come out clean.

SERVES 6–8

A Save for Every Disaster

—CATHERINE GAMMON

One night, shortly before serve-up, I was frosting twenty-three small chocolate cakes, each cake meant to serve four people, each cake resting on its own individual glass plate, when suddenly the plate in my hand had fallen and shattered, sending myriad shards of glass flying and disappearing primarily into other cakes and cake plates. The disaster was too great to waste any time wondering how it had happened. I was clueless what to do other than look around and call out for help: "Dale?"

Fortunately, Dale Kent was at hand and had seen even worse messes than this one in front of me, which he studied briefly before coming up with the solution.

The first step was to remove every plate that could conceivably have been garnished with glass, no matter if we could see glass or not. Those cakes were composted, and those plates were moved and replaced. Next step was to cut the remaining cakes into eight pieces and to arrange them in a kind of pinwheel, four pieces to a plate, and to lavish each plate with strawberries.

The solution sounds simple and almost obvious with hindsight, but in the moment of the shattering glass, with the dining room full of guests and the dining room servers ready to carry over the huge trays filled with the night's offerings, the loss seemed beyond recovery.

For me, this was the amazing moment and the point of the story: not the solution itself, but the calm and confidence with which Dale met the mess. That calm and confidence allowed him to see the solution, and this calm seeing was what I received.

From complete acceptance that what was lost was lost (whether chocolate cake or lentil soup) came the opportunity to respond creatively with what was actually at hand. In the kitchen, at least, there is always something, and I believe it is true everywhere. The hard part is accepting the sudden loss, the radical change. After that, it's a piece of cake.

FIRE
ALARM

Mexican Chocolate Cake

A hint of cinnamon makes this chocolaty dessert the perfect ending to a dinner full of chiles, corn, and beans. I like this cake simply sprinkled with a little powdered sugar. A splash of cajeta *(Mexican caramel) and a handful of toasted coconut makes this a sort of Mexican German Chocolate Cake. This recipe makes 24 cupcakes, one 9 x 13-inch sheet cake, or two 9-inch cakes that could be carefully cut into 4 layers.*

2 cups cake flour or all-purpose flour
2 teaspoons baking soda
½ teaspoon salt
1 teaspoon cinnamon
4 ounces unsweetened chocolate, chopped
    well so it melts fast
5 tablespoons cocoa powder

1¼ cups boiling water
½ cup butter
2 cups brown sugar
3 large eggs
2 teaspoons vanilla
½ cup thin yogurt or buttermilk

Preheat oven to 350 degrees.

Grease cake pans with butter and then put a thin coating of flour, sugar, or cocoa on top by throwing a tablespoon or two of one of these dry ingredients into the pan and swirling it around. The powders will stick to the grease, and you can easily see if you missed a spot.

Sift together flour, baking soda, salt, and cinnamon.

In a heatproof bowl, combine the chocolate and cocoa powder. Pour boiling water over the top and whisk until smooth.

In a large bowl, beat the butter until smooth and lighter in color, with a little more volume; continue beating and add sugar. Cream the butter and sugar together until the mixture is light and fluffy.

NOTE: *This is where you get a lot of the lift in your cake—little air bubbles beaten into suspension. When placed in the oven, the water molecules in the butter matrix will steam, the air will expand, and that is how you get a nice fluffy cake.*

Beat one egg at a time into the butter mixture. (Beating the eggs in one at a time means each egg is fully incorporated before adding the next one. This helps beat more air into your batter and helps

recipe continued on page 166

to emulsify the eggs into the butter.) If you are making a large batch of batter, you can add the eggs a few at a time.

Add the vanilla and the chocolate mixture; stir together. Add half the dry ingredients and mix to combine. Stir in the yogurt and then add the rest of the dry ingredients.

Try not to mix any more than you absolutely have to. If you are using a stand mixer, scrape the bowl and blades frequently during each addition. If you are stirring by hand, pay attention and make each swipe through the batter really count.

Pour the batter into the prepared pans and bake for 25 to 30 minutes for cupcakes and round cakes, and up to 35 or 40 minutes for a single sheet cake. A toothpick inserted into the center of the cake should come out dry and free of crumbs. If you press gently on the cake, it will spring back.

NOTE: *Most cake recipes ask you to have all the ingredients at room temperature. You want the ingredients at room temperature so they don't chill the butter. A cake batter is a tricky emulsion of fats, and it helps if everything is the same temperature. Of course, many people have made lots of successful cakes without being too picky about this, but do keep it in mind—and if you know you're going to make a cake, go ahead and take the ingredients out of the fridge in time for them to lose their chill. You'll be glad you did. If you put your uncracked eggs in a bowl and pour some warm (not boiling!) water over them, they will warm up in just a few minutes.*

NOTE: *For generations, boiling a can of sweetened condensed milk has been a shortcut to making cajeta, a classic caramelized milk confection. Traditionally, it was simply made with fresh milk that was cooked down to one-third or less of its volume over a long period of time. The natural sugars begin to break down and caramelize, and the resulting sweet milk has a much longer shelf life than fresh milk. Indian cooks also make desserts like kheer, kulfi, and halva out of milk that is cooked down over a number of hours. Boiling a can of sweetened condensed milk can be dangerous. If there is any air in the can it could explode. The safer method: pour the condensed milk into a heavy-bottom pot and cook over medium-low heat for 30 minutes or so. You can cook it in a double boiler if you don't want to pay attention and stir regularly.*

SERVES ABOUT 12

Chocolate Mousse

This mousse is velvety and rich and always a favorite with chocolate lovers. It uses a sabayon, in which you whisk eggs, sugar, and a little water, liqueur, or wine together over a double boiler until a beautiful pale foam is created. One advantage of this is that the eggs are cooked, and so you avoid potential risks associated with raw eggs. Making a sabayon requires a lot of whisking, but it is worth the effort. You can experiment with different kinds of chocolate and liqueurs to vary the flavor.

10 ounces bittersweet chocolate	2 egg yolks
20 ounces heavy cream	¼ cup sugar
2 eggs	½ ounce Grand Marnier or other liqueur

Melt the chocolate over a double boiler; keep warm and ready.

Whip the cream until soft peaks form; keep in the refrigerator until ready to use.

Combine the eggs, yolks, sugar, and liqueur in a double boiler. Whisk constantly until the mixture is pale and densely foamy. Gently fold the melted chocolate into the egg mixture. Fold in one-third of the whipped cream to lighten the egg and chocolate mixture. Gently fold in the remaining whipped cream until the mousse is completely mixed together. With a pastry bag, fill the intended serving containers. Refrigerate for 2 hours.

SERVES 4–6

Chocolate-Dipped Strawberries

This is a timeless and easy dessert preparation, and the combination of strawberries and chocolate is both rich and refreshing. The process of preparing chocolate for dipping, known as tempering, can be used for a variety of cookies and fruit or other desserts. For variation, you can try figs, pineapple, kiwi, or melon. Tempering chocolate is not hard or mysterious. It just requires a gentle and patient hand.

2 pounds good-quality bittersweet chocolate

Strawberries, clean and dry

Chop the chocolate into small pieces. This helps the chocolate melt quickly and evenly.

Melt two thirds of the chocolate over a double boiler. The water in the bottom pan should be gently simmering. Avoid getting any water in the chocolate as this will make it harden instantly. Heat the chocolate until it just melts. If the chocolate hardens, you may be able to rescue it with a tablespoon or two of butter stirred into the melted chocolate.

Add most of the unmelted chocolate to the melted chocolate and begin stirring with a wooden spoon. The unmelted chocolate will begin to cool the melted chocolate and will provide the necessary fat crystals to temper the chocolate. Stir continously as the chocolate cools. You will probably need to stir for 5 to 10 minutes.

Test the temper by dipping a clean knife into the chocolate. The chocolate should harden in less than 5 minutes and should look shiny and have no white streaks in it. If the chocolate is not quite ready, add a little more of the unmelted chocolate and continue stirring. Test again in a couple of minutes.

When the chocolate is ready, dip the strawberries and set on a platter or baking sheet. If the chocolate cools or gets too thick, you can warm it for 3 seconds over the burner on the stove and give it a stir to distribute the heat. Leftover chocolate can be poured onto parchment or a baking sheet to cool and then reused for any recipe.

The strawberries can be dipped ahead of time and kept cool in the refrigerator, especially in the hot days of summer.

Chocolate Ganache

Ganache is a really versatile chocolate product that is easy to make and very forgiving. Basically, ganache is equal parts (by weight, not volume) cream and chocolate. A ganache with a higher ratio of chocolate to cream is harder and more dense than a ganache with less chocolate. These firm ganaches will hold their shape well and are used as a truffle filling. Soft ganache makes a really easy frosting for a cake. You can flavor this basic ganache with just about anything. A little Grand Marnier is especially nice, but vanilla extract or almond essence are nice nonalcoholic alternatives.

8 ounces chocolate (60 percent cacao works well, but both darker and lighter chocolates also work)

1 cup heavy cream
1 tablespoon vanilla (or flavoring of choice)

Chop the chocolate into small pieces and put in a heatproof bowl. Heat the cream almost to a boil and pour it over the chocolate. Add vanilla and stir well until the chocolate is melted and the ganache is smooth and thick. This can be poured over a cake before it cools. Or put it in a bowl over ice and whisk it if you want to thicken it up to spread a thicker layer over your cake. If you whisk it really well for a few minutes or longer, it will become more light and fluffy—a nice filling for cream puffs.

NOTE: *Julia Child says that if you use twice the amount of cream and whip it well, you can make an easy chocolate mousse. Freeze this mixture for ice cream.*

NOTE: *Ganache is really easy to work with and fun to use. Harold McGee says that the word is French for "cushion." His description of the recipe and final product is as follows: "To make ganache, the cream is scalded and the chocolate melted into it to form a complex combination of an emulsion and a suspension. The continuous phase of this mixture, the portion that permeates it, is a syrup made from the cream's water and the chocolate's sugar. Suspended in the syrup are the milk fat globules from the cream, and cocoa butter droplets and solid cocoa particles from the chocolate." Isn't cooking amazing?*

MAKES ENOUGH FOR 1 CAKE

Almond Biscotti

A lot of biscotti recipes are cooked without any butter, but that little bit of extra fat provides a nice tenderness. If you like those really crisp, hard cookies that demand a cup of coffee or a glass of wine for dunking, just omit the butter. They are drier and crunchier without the butter and their shelf life is considerably longer.

1½ cups almonds	1½ cups sugar
3 cups all-purpose flour	3 eggs
1¼ teaspoons baking powder	¾ teaspoon vanilla extract
⅓ teaspoon salt	⅓ teaspoon almond extract
4 tablespoons butter, softened	Zest from 1 lemon (optional)

Toast the almonds at 350 degrees until they are starting to darken a bit and beginning to smell nice and nutty; let cool and then chop coarsely.

In a bowl, combine the flour, baking powder, and salt with a wire whisk to mix well.

In a separate bowl, cream the butter and sugar together until smooth and a little fluffy. Add the eggs one at a time, beating thoroughly before each addition. (This further aerates the batter and helps establish a nice network of protein and fat to provide structure for the trapped air that will expand in the heat of the oven.)

Stir in the extracts and lemon zest. Sprinkle half of the flour mixture over the surface of the egg mixture and give the batter a few quick strokes to fold it in. There should still be streaks of dry flour when you add the second half of the flour. Mix in the remaining flour mixture and stir in the almonds until just combined.

Line two baking sheets with parchment paper, or butter the surface to prevent sticking. Divide the dough into 3 or 4 parts. With lightly floured hands on a lightly floured board, roll and pull the dough into 1- to 2-inch-wide logs. Bake the logs at least 2 inches apart on the prepared pans at 350 degrees for 25 to 30 minutes. They should have risen and no longer be wet in the center when you give them a gentle nudge with a finger. Cracks will have formed, and the logs will be starting to brown on the surface. Turn the oven down to 325 degrees. Take the logs out of the oven and let them cool for 5 to 10 minutes before you slice them and bake them again. "Biscotti" means "twice cooked" and this is why. You bake them through in log form and then complete the cooking after slicing the logs into individual cookies.

The logs are very tender and fragile when they are warm, so you might want to use a couple of big spatulas or very large, gentle hands to transfer the baked loaves to a cutting board. Cut the loaves in slices about ½ inch thick. If you cut them at a slight angle, the cookies will be longer than if you cut them straight across. Set them out on the cookie sheets with about ½ inch between each cookie so they can dry out. Bake for 7 or 8 minutes and then flip. Bake for another 7 or 8 minutes until the cookies are lightly browned on both sides.

SERVES 8–12

Sweet Coconut Rice

This sweet sticky rice is a great base for any fruit. Traditionally, ripe mangos or bananas would be sliced fresh and served on top of a serving of this rice for a soothing dessert. Use whatever fruit is fresh, local, and at the height of its season. Peaches, pears, and berries are all delicious with this dessert. Make sure to toss peaches or pears with a little lemon juice to keep them from turning brown.

2 cups glutinous (sweet) rice
2½ cups coconut milk

⅔ cup sugar
Pinch of salt

Soak rice overnight in plenty of cool, clean water. Drain rice and steam over boiling water in a steamer basket lined with cheesecloth. Cook for 20 to 25 minutes, or until the center of a grain of rice is no longer chalky and hard. Put the rice in a saucepan and add the coconut milk, sugar, and salt. Simmer covered over very low heat until the coconut milk is absorbed. Stir occasionally as it cooks to keep it from sticking.

SERVES 6–8

Pear-Quince Compote

Quince is a hard tart fruit that is popular in Persian cuisine. They are usually not available until September. Any nice firm pear or even Golden Delicious apples are a fine substitute.

3 cups quince*	2 tablespoons honey (lighter type is best)
3 cups pears*	½ vanilla bean, split and scraped
1 cup water	1 cinnamon stick
½ cup white wine	½ cup toasted and chopped almonds
½ cup sugar	

Peel and slice the quince and pears. Do not combine.

In a 2-quart saucepan, combine the water, wine, sugar, and honey. Bring mixture to a boil and stir until sugar is dissolved. Add the vanilla bean, cinnamon stick, and the quince. Reduce heat to a simmer and cook for 18 minutes. Add the pears and continue to cook for another 15 minutes. Using a slotted spoon, remove the fruit to a serving dish. Remove vanilla bean and cinnamon stick, and boil the juices until reduced by half. Pour reduced liquid over the fruit. Garnish with the almonds. Top with whipped cream, if desired.

*Use all pears or any combination of pears and quince to equal 6 cups.

SERVES 4–6

Strawberry Pie

This sweet and delicious pie goes well with a nice dollop of unsweetened plain yogurt or crème fraîche.

CRUST

1½ cups graham cracker crumbs

6 tablespoons melted butter

¼ cup sugar

FILLING

6 cups halved or quartered ripe
strawberries, divided

1 cup sugar

¼ cup cornstarch

Pinch of salt

½ cup water

2 tablespoons fresh lemon juice

Preheat oven to 350 degrees.

For the crust, lightly oil a 9-inch pie pan. Mix together the graham cracker crumbs, butter, and sugar. Press the mixture into the pie pan to form a crust. Bake for 12 to 15 minutes, or until the crust is fragrant and lightly browned; cool.

For the filling, purée 2 cups strawberries, setting aside the rest. Transfer the strawberry purée to a saucepan. Add sugar, cornstarch, salt, water, and lemon juice. Bring the mixture to a simmer over medium-high heat, stirring constantly until thickened, about 1 minute. Fill the crust with remaining berries and top with the strawberry purée; chill until set.

SERVES 6–8

Lemon Sponge Custard with Raspberry Sauce

This dessert is a perennial favorite at Tassajara. It is especially wonderful in the summer when Meyer lemons are available. Try to serve it warm from the oven if you can. The texture is amazing, and there is a little bit of a soufflé-like puff that falls within 10 or 15 minutes.

CUSTARD

1½ tablespoons butter, softened
¾ cup sugar
2 teaspoons lemon zest
3 eggs, separated

3 tablespoons sifted all-purpose flour
¼ cup lemon juice
1 cup milk

SAUCE

1 pint raspberries
3 tablespoons confectioners' sugar

2 tablespoons orange liqueur or orange
    flower water
½ teaspoon almond extract

Preheat the oven to 350 degrees.

For the custard, cream together the butter, sugar, and zest. Beat the egg yolks, add to sugar mixture, and beat well. Stir in the flour alternately with the lemon juice and milk.

Beat the egg whites until stiff but not dry. Fold them into the yolk mixture. Place the batter in a buttered 7-inch baking or casserole dish. Set on a rack in a pan filled with 1 inch of hot water. Bake about 1 hour, or until set. The edges of the sponge will start to pull away from the sides of the casserole, and the top will begin to turn golden.

For the sauce, blend together all the ingredients in a blender or food processor; strain through a sieve, pressing firmly with a rubber spatula. Taste and add sugar and/or flavorings. Spoon over the custard servings.

VARIATION: *Orange Sponge Custard*
Use the same recipe, above, substituting 1 tablespoon orange zest for the lemon zest, and ½ cup orange juice for the lemon juice. Add ¼ teaspoon to ½ teaspoon of ground cardamom with the flour.

SERVES 4–6

Peach Pie

Peach pie at the height of the harvest season is a treat like no other. If you do not have quite enough ripe peaches, mix in some berries, cherries, or apricots.

Pie crust recipe, for a double crust (see page 151)

FILLING

½ cup sugar

⅛ teaspoon salt

1½ tablespoons cornstarch

⅛ teaspoon nutmeg

¼ teaspoon ground cardamom

½ teaspoon lemon zest

5 to 6 cups sliced peaches

1½ to 2 tablespoons butter

1 tablespoon lemon juice

Water or egg wash

1 teaspoon cinnamon sugar (½ teaspoon of each mixed together)

For the crust, prepare the dough and line a 9-inch pie pan with half. Roll out the other half into a 10-inch disk. Pierce it with a fork or cut out little shapes with a small cookie cutter to allow steam to escape when you bake the pie. For a lattice crust, roll dough into a 9 x 12-inch rectangle and cut twelve equal strips. Line up 6 strips on the counter with about ½ inch between them. Fold every other strip in half towards you and lay down one of the other six strips perpendicularly to the strips on the counter. Fold back the three strips over the top and repeat, using all strips to create a lattice top. Place top crust on a sheet of parchment paper and keep it cool until you need it.

Preheat oven to 425 degrees.

For the filling, combine the sugar, salt, cornstarch, spices, and zest, and sprinkle over the peaches. Gently stir the peaches to coat them with the sugar mixture. Place the peaches in the pie shell and dot with little pieces of butter. Sprinkle lemon juice over the peaches. Brush the edges of the dough with a little water or egg wash and lay the top crust over the peaches. Tuck the edge of the top crust under the edge of the bottom crust. Pinch all the way around the edges to seal the crust and make a decorative fluted edge. Brush top with egg wash or lemon juice and sprinkle with cinnamon sugar. Bake at 425 degrees for 10 minutes, then reduce the heat to 350 degrees and continue baking until the filling is beginning to bubble up and the crust is golden brown, about 35 to 45 minutes.

SERVES 6–8

Shortcake

These shortcakes are really a slightly sweetened biscuit, and they make the perfect base for summer fruits and berries. The secret to making them is to keep your ingredients cold and to not work the dough too much after the cream is added, only enough to make it come together. They are best served warm out of the oven.

2 cups all-purpose flour	½ teaspoon salt
2 teaspoons baking powder	½ cup unsalted butter
2 tablespoons sugar	¾ to 1 cup heavy whipping cream

In a bowl, mix together the flour, baking powder, sugar, and salt. Starting with ½-inch cubes of cold butter, cut it into the flour mixture with two knives, or by rubbing the butter and flour together with your fingers. Continue until the mixture resembles course cornmeal. It's okay to have some smaller lumps of butter remaining.

Make a well in the center of the flour mixture and add the cream. Mix just enough to bring the dough together. Turn it onto a floured board and knead together a half dozen times. Roll out to ¾ inch thick, and cut into squares, circles, diamonds, or any shape you like. By gently pressing the scraps together, you can cut a few more shortcakes. Place the shortcakes on an ungreased baking sheet. Brush the tops with some cream. Bake in a 425-degree oven until the tops are lightly brown, about 12 to 15 minutes; cool on a rack.

SERVES 4–6

Fruit Crisp

For this recipe, you can use whatever nuts are around—at least two but not more than three kinds together. Almonds and walnuts are a favorite, but try using hazelnuts and cashews if you are feeling rich. Pistachios are nice with almonds for apricots and peaches. Pecans are used in most crisp toppings in Texas. Chop the nuts together in a food processor, but stop before the grind gets too fine or powdery— you want some chunks and texture.

½ cup white sugar

½ cup brown sugar

½ teaspoon nutmeg

½ teaspoon cinnamon

¼ teaspoon allspice

⅛ teaspoon salt

1 cup all-purpose flour

½ cup butter, cut into thin slabs and kept cold or frozen*

¾ to 1 cup coarsely chopped mixed nuts

¾ cups rolled oats

6 to 8 cups sliced ripe fruit

1 to 4 tablespoons sugar (optional)

Preheat oven to 375 degrees.

Butter an 8 x 10-inch baking dish or a 2-quart casserole dish. In a large bowl, mix together the sugars, spices, salt, and flour. Toss the butter together with the dry ingredients. Working as quickly as you can with your hands, rub and press the butter into the flour mixture just until it starts to hold together. Mix in the nuts and the oats, and then chill while you prepare the fruit. Put the fruit in the prepared baking dish. Taste the fruit and toss with a little sugar if it seems to need it (remember the topping is awfully sweet already!). Sprinkle the topping over the fruit. Gently press the crumb topping down, but be careful not to press it into a dense slab. It is quite a thick layer of topping, not just a smattering, and it needs to be lightly compressed but still have a little air to breath in the heat of the oven. Bake for 25 to 50 minutes until the fruit is bubbling and the topping is lightly browned and crisp. Cooking time depends on the type and temperature of the fruit, the size of the pan, the true heat of the oven, and many other factors too numerous to mention.

Substitute soy margarine or coconut oil and a little exotic nut oil for a vegan version, which tends to be a little less crisp.

SERVES 6–8

Olive Oil Date Cake

This cake recipe is a variation of Deborah Madison's Olive Oil Cake from Vegetarian Cooking for Everyone *(1997). She recommends calling this a chiffon cake because "people often balk at the idea, but not the taste, of an olive oil cake."*

According to the folks at Cook's Illustrated, *the first chiffon cake was invented in 1927 by a man named Harry Baker. He baked forty-two cakes a day to sell to the Brown Derby restaurant. He kept the recipe to himself for 20 years before selling it to General Mills. In 1948, a little booklet with variations, recipes, frostings, and fillings called* Betty Crocker Chiffon *was released. At the time, cake recipes using vegetable oil instead of butter were sort of a novelty.*

4 eggs, separated, plus 1 extra egg white	½ teaspoon freshly grated nutmeg
½ teaspoon cream of tartar	¼ teaspoon ground cloves
1 cup brown sugar, packed	1⅓ cups milk or almond milk
2½ cups cake flour	½ cup plus 2 tablespoons olive oil
2 teaspoons baking powder	1 teaspoon vanilla
½ teaspoon salt	¾ cup chopped dates
2 teaspoons cinnamon	Confectioners' sugar

Preheat the oven to 375 degrees. Butter and flour a 10-inch springform or Bundt pan.

Separate the eggs while they are cold because the fat of the yolk is more solid and easier to separate. Let the whites come to room temperature, or heat gently over a pan of warm water before whipping them so that they have more volume than if they are cold.

Beat the egg whites in a large clean bowl until soft peaks form. Add the cream of tartar and continue whipping until firm peaks form and begin to lose their shine or look dry. This is farther than you would normally take the beating of a meringue, but it is a little more stable product to fold into the flour mixture. Transfer the egg whites into a bowl.

Sift the sugar, flour, baking powder, salt, cinnamon, nutmeg, and cloves into the same bowl you beat the whites in. Whisk the egg yolks, milk, oil, and vanilla together, then whisk into the dry ingredients. Be careful not to overmix the flour. Stir only until the batter is smooth. Fold in the egg whites, making sure that all the pockets of thick meringue get broken up by breaking them down with the side of the spatula. Arrange chopped dates artfully on the bottom of the pan or fold them quickly into the batter.

Pour the batter into the prepared pan and bake for 20 minutes. Reduce the temperature to 325 degrees and continue baking for another 45 minutes, or until the cake begins pulling away from the sides of the pan and a toothpick comes out clean. Deborah Madison says that it is better to overbake this cake than underbake it. When the cake cools, give it a dusting of powdered sugar and serve.

SERVES 6–8

Don't Forget the Sugar
—GLORIA LEE

I asked my dessert cook for sixteen small rounds of chocolate cake. When I tasted one of the beautifully baked and cooled cakes, I knew something was wrong. They weren't very sweet! We went over the recipe and found she had used 2 cups sugar instead of 8. This is a common mistake in the early phase of volume cooking.

I decided to make them into layer cakes with a raspberry jam filling. Then I also spread a thin coating of jam on top of the cake and finished it with finely chopped walnuts. At this point the raspberry-chocolate cakes were sweet enough for dessert.

However, I was surprised when guests at two tables asked for the recipe. I told them it was a complicated process and directed them to a local cookbook.

Marzipan-Stuffed Dates

Although one could presumably use any type of date for this uncomplicated yet very elegant sweet to end a North African or Mediterranean feast, voluptuous Medjool dates work best. After laboring on more complicated savory parts of a meal, the minimalist preparation required of this dessert allows one to create a beautiful platter with cleaved pomegranates, bunches of black grapes, fresh figs, or oranges, depending on the season, in very little time.

16 dates
3 to 8 tablespoons marzipan or almond paste

Simply draw a lengthwise incision with a sharp knife across the top of each date and remove the pit, keeping the date intact. Soften the marzipan by quickly pulsing it in a food processor or massaging portions of it in your hands. You may wish to add a few drops of rose water or orange flower water or flecks of citrus zest to give the paste a distinct aromatic flavor. Creating small almond-shaped rounds, fill each date to desired capacity. If you choose to reveal the almond paste, consider adorning it with a pistachio nut, pomegranate seed, or orange calendula petal to offset the brown date. Otherwise, reseal the date and leave the paste a hidden surprise for your guest to discover as he or she bites into it.

VARIATIONS

A different variation for this dessert is to stuff the Medjools with goat cheese—the slight tang of the cheese nicely complements the honey-like sweetness of the dates. Another delicious variation is to fill the dates with Italian mascarpone cheese mixed with slivers of crystallized ginger. This last variation, rich and unusual, will surely delight everyone.

SERVES 6–8

Cardamom Carrot Cake

The combination of cardamom, ginger, cinnamon, and cloves gives this carrot cake a satisfying and unique flavor. Frost it with a cream cheese frosting if you like, but it is fine with just a simple dusting of powdered sugar.

1 pound carrots, grated

1 cup granulated sugar, divided

2½ cups all-purpose flour (unbleached)

1¼ teaspoons baking powder

1 teaspoon baking soda

1 teaspoon cinnamon

1 teaspoon ground cardamom seeds

⅛ teaspoon cloves

½ teaspoon salt

1 cup brown sugar

4 eggs

1½ cups safflower or canola oil

Toss the carrots in a colander over a bowl with ½ cup sugar; let rest in the bowl for at least 15 minutes. (This helps the carrots release a lot of their water and leads to less dense, waterlogged cake.) Preheat the oven to 350 degrees and butter and flour a 9 x 13-inch baking pan or two 9-inch round cake pans.

Whisk together the flour, baking powder, baking soda, cinnamon, cardamon, cloves, and salt. In a separate bowl, beat together the remaining granulated sugar with the brown sugar, eggs, and oil. Stir the carrots into the egg mixture and gently combine with the flour until well mixed with no pockets of flour left dry. Pour the batter into the prepared pan(s) and bake for 30 to 40 minutes. A toothpick inserted in the center of the cake should come out clean. Cool cake in the pan for at least a couple of hours.

SERVES 6–8

*Ricotta Chevre with Ginger
Berry Compote*

Ricotta Chevre with Ginger Berry Compote

This is a very simple dessert best served with a nice light meal at the height of berry season. If using strawberries, leave out the ginger.

Ricotta cheese	Sugar
Goat cheese	Grated fresh ginger
Fresh berries	Mint sprigs

In a bowl, beat equal parts ricotta cheese and goat cheese until well combined. Form by hand into 2- to 3-inch-wide patties. If you have more than a couple of pounds of cheese, use an ice cream scoop to portion it out and then pat the scoops into saucer shapes.

Rinse the freshest berries you can find and toss them with a few tablespoons of sugar and a teaspoon of freshly grated ginger per pint of berries. Heat the berries in a saucepan for about 10 minutes over medium heat until they begin to release their juices and start to break down. Ladle warm compote over the cheese disks and garnish with a sprig of mint.

Lucy's Mochi Cake

This is a Westernized baked version of a Chinese New Year's cake. Traditionally it's steamed or fried. If sweetened red bean paste isn't to your liking, make a sweetened peanut, sesame, or date paste instead.

1 can or 1 to 1½ pounds red bean paste (sweetened)	1 cup light vegetable oil
1 pound sweet rice flour (Mochiko is a widely-available brand)	3 eggs or ¼ cup oil
½ to 1 cup sugar, adjust to taste	2½ cups milk or rice milk
	1 teaspoon baking powder

Grease a 9 x 13-inch baking dish. Spread red bean paste evenly on the bottom of the pan. Beat all other ingredients together in a bowl until well combined. Spread batter on top of the red beans. Bake for 1 hour at 350 degrees.

SERVES 12

Rice Pudding with Cinnamon, Cardamom, and Vanilla

The Buddha broke his fast under the bodhi tree with a bowl of rice pudding. While we can't guarantee any sort of supreme perfect enlightenment will come from this recipe, it sure is a delicious treat.

2 cups water
1 cup white basmati rice
¼ teaspoon salt
4 cups whole milk
1 cup whipping cream

⅔ cup sugar
1 teaspoon ground cinnamon
½ teaspoon ground cardamom
1½ teaspoons vanilla extract

Boil the water in a large heavy-bottom saucepan. Pour in the rice and salt, give it a quick stir, and cover the pot. Simmer over low heat for about 15 to 20 minutes. Stir a few times while it cooks. Add the remaining ingredients except for the vanilla. Turn the heat up and bring the pudding to a simmer. When it begins to simmer, turn the heat down so the pudding is maintained at a simmer. Simmer uncovered for about 30 minutes, then turn the heat down to low and continue cooking for about 15 minutes more, or until the mixture is thick. Stir frequently, making sure the pudding is not sticking to the bottom of the pot. When done, stir in the vanilla and enjoy warm or cold. A skin will form on the surface if you do not cover it with plastic wrap.

SERVES 6–8

Coconut Custard with Lychees

A simple and tasty finish to a Thai or Asian fusion meal.

4 eggs, beaten
½ cup plus 1 tablespoon sugar
¼ teaspoon salt
2 (14-ounce) cans coconut milk
½ cup shredded unsweetened coconut

1 (20-ounce) can lychees (found in most grocery stores)
1 tablespoon sugar
1 vanilla bean or a few drops of vanilla extract
Mint leaves for garnish

Preheat oven to 300 degrees. Grease 6 ramekins or a 9-inch baking dish.

Whisk together the eggs, ½ cup sugar, salt, and coconut milk in a bowl. Pour into ramekins or a baking dish. Place in the oven in a deep pan. Add hot water to the pan until the water level comes two-thirds up the side of the ramekins or baking dish to create a bain-marie (water bath). Bake 35 minutes for the ramekins or 1 hour for a baking dish, or until a knife stuck in the center comes out clean; set aside to cool.

While the custard is baking, toast the coconut in a pan on the stove until browned. Drain the lychees and reserve the syrup. Boil the syrup with 1 tablespoon sugar and vanilla bean or vanilla extract on the stove until the syrup has thickened. Remove the vanilla bean, if using, and set syrup aside to cool. Chop the lychees into small pieces. To serve, sprinkle the lychees and toasted coconut on top of the custard and pour the syrup over the top. Garnish with mint leaves.

SERVES 6–8

Sweet Tapioca Soup with Honeydew

At Tassajara we serve this dessert soup with Thai, Chinese, and Japanese meals. As desserts go, it requires very little work.

¼ cup small pearl tapioca
1 cup water
2 cups coconut milk

4 to 6 tablespoons sugar
1 cup milk
1 large, ripe honeydew melon

Soak the tapioca in the water for about 45 minutes. Drain the tapioca and combine it with the coconut milk and sugar. Heat over medium heat until it begins to thicken. Pour in the milk and let this mixture cool. (It will form a skin on the surface if you don't cover it with plastic wrap.)

Cut the honeydew melon into chunks and purée in a food processor or chop very fine. Combine the honeydew with the tapioca mixture and chill.

SERVES 6–8

Melon with Mint and Candied Ginger

This is a light refreshing dessert salad that goes well at the end of a heavy meal. The recipe came about when we got a case of honeydew melons that were not sweet enough for the dessert we had planned—an elegant plate with walnuts, candied ginger, and slices of perfectly ripe melon. We made this simple salad instead of serving mediocre melon, and it has been a favorite ever since.

1 tablespoon candied ginger
2 tablespoons mint
1 to 2 tablespoons sugar

Juice of 1 lemon
1 fresh melon, seeded, sectioned, and
    cut into bite-size pieces

Chop the ginger with the mint until it forms a dry paste. Dissolve sugar in lemon juice and marinate the ginger and mint paste in it for a few minutes before tossing with the cut melon.

SERVES 4

Sweet Tapioca Soup with Honeydew

Maccha Truffles

This brilliant recipe came to Tassajara from Eric Gower, a private chef in San Francisco and the author of The Breakaway Japanese Kitchen *(2003) and* The Breakaway Cook *(2007). In April 2007, he came to do a weekend-long workshop with the guest-cooks-in-training. During those two days, Eric generously shared his recipes and an enthusiasm for creating unusual combinations that blend simple ingredients with the flavors of maccha tea, pomegranate molasses, umeboshi, and a variety of flavored salts, among other things.*

1 cup heavy cream	12 ounces bittersweet chocolate,
¼ cup maple syrup	finely chopped
2 tablespoons brown sugar	Pinch of maccha salt or kosher salt
2 tablespoons maccha, divided	

Bring the cream to a simmer in a small saucepan over gentle heat. Add the maple syrup and brown sugar, and stir until dissolved, about 2 minutes. Add 1 tablespoon maccha, stirring until dissolved; set aside.

Place the chocolate in a large mixing bowl and pour in the cream mixture. Mix thoroughly and pour onto a baking sheet lined with parchment paper; smooth with a rubber spatula. Cool in the refrigerator for about 1 hour. Scoop out a heaping teaspoonful and make a ball using your palms. Repeat until all the chocolate is used—you should end up with about 50 truffles. Line them up on a tray or plate and dust them with the remaining tablespoon of maccha, using a fine sieve. Top with a very light sprinkling of maccha salt.

NOTE: *Maccha is powdered green tea from Japan. If you cannot find it at a local store, go to www.japanesegreenteaonline.com. It is usually sold in small tins that cost around 12 to 14 dollars for about 1 ounce. This is a very special product that we use only occasionally at Tassajara. Generally, it is reserved for tea ceremonies and special guests, but these little gems certainly warrant the use of this precious substance.*

Maccha salt is simply maccha and sea salt whirred together in a coffee grinder. It adds a brilliant green accent and a slight bitterness that complements all sorts of food from carrots to eggs to chocolate.

MAKES ABOUT 50 TRUFFLES

Chocolate Chunk Cookies

These cookies studded with big pieces of chocolate beat the original Toll House cookie by a mile.

1¼ cups flour
½ teaspoon baking powder
½ teaspoon baking soda
½ teaspoon salt
1 stick butter, room temperature
¾ cup light brown sugar

1 large egg, room temperature
1 teaspoon vanilla
1 cup 70 percent bittersweet chocolate, cut
    into shards and chunks
1 cup pecans, chopped in large pieces

Preheat the oven to 375 degrees.

Mix the first four ingredients together in a bowl. Cream the butter and sugar until light and fluffy, about 2 minutes in an electric mixer; add the egg and vanilla, and beat until smooth. Scrape down the sides at least once to make sure everything is well incorporated. With the mixer on low, add the dry ingredients. When thoroughly mixed, add the chocolate and nuts. Mound heaping teaspoons of the cookie dough on sheet pans, leaving about 2 inches between each mound. Bake in the center of the oven (rotate pans if you're using two shelves) for 10 minutes, or until lightly browned both on top and on bottom. Let cool before packing or eating.

MAKES ABOUT 2 DOZEN COOKIES

Making Cookies

—DEBORAH MADISON

When I was guest cook, our large crew did all the cutting, chopping, and slicing for the day. It was very intense and there was no time for standing around and wondering what was next.

One day I'd wanted to make Toll House cookies for the guests, but we didn't have any chocolate chips on hand. After some quick thinking, we decided to just chunk up a slab of chocolate instead. I had never heard of anyone doing this, but it was a practical solution to our problem. But what a solution! Big chunks of good-quality chocolate and pecans beat the original Toll House cookie by a mile. I don't think I've used a chocolate chip since!

The Benefits of Watermelon

—EDWARD BROWN

Once a student asked the master, "What about the student who leaves the monastery and does not return?"

"He is a horse's ass," replied the master.

"What about the student who leaves the monastery and later returns?"

"He remembers the benefits."

"What are the benefits?" the student queried.

"Heat in the summer and cold in the winter."

Perhaps this is dry Zen humor, but it is also a wonderful answer, to be reminded that there is a benefit, a simple beauty in the way things are. Not that I always understood or appreciated this when I was actually living at Tassajara. Up to a point, certainly, but heat and cold were often a torment.

At times, the usual conceptions of heat and cold were inadequate to describe what we experienced, and so the words lost their meaning. One summer working in the old kitchen, I found out how relative heat can be. During one hot spell, the temperature was over 115 degrees. This heat met the body head-on. It was no longer just the surrounding environment but an independent presence, a being that licked at our faces and pushed its body up against ours, took hold of us, and squeezed out our vitality.

The kitchen was hotter by 10 degrees or more than the baking outdoors. Sweat would pour down our faces and soak through our clothes. We'd walk outside every now and again to cool off. So what was hot? What had been sticky and oppressive a few minutes earlier was now cool and breezy. "Hot" had lost its relevance. Hot compared to what? This morning, last winter? A few degrees less, and it would still be "hot." Twenty degrees less and it would still be "hot."

Everything in the world was the world of heat. Doorknobs felt different—no longer solid but alive and pulsing. Large stones seemed to breathe. Here and there the air would shimmer and vibrate with reflected heat, making objects look twisted and wavy-edged.

The little voice that liked to whine "If it was just a little cooler . . . then it would be alright" was silenced. Awe took over. Incredulousness. Adventurousness. The response to that dear little voice would come back loud and clear. "If it was just a little cooler, you'd still be hot! So forget it." Here was hot that could not be escaped, hot that transcended hot.

One late summer day, Roovan, the gardener, and I took advantage of the heat to have a special dinner. Roovan had somehow gotten hold of a large watermelon, and he offered to share it with me.

"Let's have dinner," he said.

"Just watermelon?" I asked.

"Sure," he replied, "what could be better?"

To make it a real dinner though, we agreed to have "courses." We sat outside where we could spit out the seeds in a civilized fashion and began our meal with some thin slices for hors d'oeuvres, then some wide wedges for "soup."

"Are you ready for the entree?" Roovan wanted to know. "Let's have watermelon steaks."

So we cut big thick rounds for the entree. Sure was delicious: juicy, fragrant, sweet, succulent, that slight crispness that dissolved away into elixir.

Our hands and faces dripped, the rinds piled up. "Now let's have some salad." The pieces got more misshapen. "How about dessert?" "Would you like some coffee?" We cut out lengthy cylinders for after-dinner cigars. "Brandy?"

The world appears in infinite forms and shapes that we could never imagine, often beyond the limits of what we consider comfortable or pleasant. To find benefit in the way things are frees us from trying to make everything conform to our standards. Like watermelon on a hot day—what a relief.

basic techniques

Cooking Basics

At Tassajara, the first thing we do when we go to the kitchen is wash our hands. Every single time. Even if you just washed your hands in the restroom. Wash them again. And wash them well.

Wash your hands with hot soapy water. You should actively wash under flowing water for a full 15 seconds. That's a very long time to stand and wring your hands together. A full quarter of a minute. During that time, use a nail brush to scrub your fingernails and really rub your hands together.

Soap is not a magic substance. Soap merely helps water emulsify the oils on your skin so that they can be washed off along with any little microscopic beasties. Soap doesn't do any cleaning on its own. It just helps you use water more efficiently.

Wash your hands frequently throughout the day. If you just carried a produce box that sat in fields and rode on the back of a truck through Salinas, you need to wash your hands before you handle food. Whenever you touch your hair or face, you should wash your hands. As an offering to your health and the health of all beings, please make washing your hands a habit that you return to religiously throughout a shift in your kitchen.

As you wash your hands you can take a few deep breaths. Clear your mind for 15 seconds—just a quarter of a minute—before you cook, and you'll be able to listen to your body and your food. The walls of your kitchen will echo with the silence that you were able to access.

In *Bendowa, The Wholehearted Way*, Dogen says that when we cultivate silence, we "universally help the Buddha work" everywhere. These moments when we can lose ourselves are essential for our well-being and the well-being of the whole world. Try to give a few moments to simply breathing deeply and dropping off all of your mental activity. Dogen says that we do this "because earth, grasses and trees, fences and walls, tiles and pebbles, all things in the dharma realm in ten directions, carry out Buddha work, therefore everyone receives the benefit of wind and water movement caused by this . . . and all are imperceptibly helped by the wondrous and incomprehensible influence of Buddha to actualize the enlightenment at hand."

ROASTING

Roasting is the most delicious way to cook starchy root vegetables (potatoes, parsnips, carrots, yams, and rutabagas). The long cooking time helps to break the carbohydrates down into simple sugars. When this happens, the vegetables brown and then caramelize. No other cooking method achieves such depth of flavor with so little work. It's very easy.

Toss vegetables in a little oil, salt, and pepper and throw them on a sheet pan in a 375-degree oven. You are now free to do a lot of other things before you need to spend any more time with the vegetables transforming inside the oven.

Coating vegetables with oil before you roast them helps them cook faster. The air molecules in the oven bombard whatever you put in the oven and transfer their stored heat to the veggies. If they meet a layer of oil, their energy is transformed into raising the heat of the oil. If they meet water molecules sweating out of veggies, the energy will just turn directly into steam, lowering the heat of the air in the oven rather than raising the heat of the vegetables. The oil helps the moisture stay in; the veggies cook faster and hotter, and end up being oh so juicy, delicious, and sweet.

SAUTÉING

"Sauté" comes from the French word meaning to "jump." Traditionally, sautéing is a dry frying technique with small amounts of food in a pan that is kept constantly moving. The heat is transferred quickly to each morsel of food.

Coat vegetables with a little oil for richness and to seal in the interior moisture. Start by heating a sauté pan. Then add a little bit of oil. Sprinkle in a little salt and some cut veggies.

NOTE: *If you try to sauté too many vegetables at a time, they will steam rather than getting the quicker, hotter heat that you're going for.*

Cook over high heat, stirring constantly. Sautéed vegetables can be cooked to any degree of doneness.

Sometimes it's nice to sauté vegetables that have already been blanched or partially cooked. Sautéing blanched green beans gives them a nice brown finish.

SAUTÉ VARIATIONS

Add a little liquid after a while and steam your vegetables the rest of the way.

Stick vegetables in the oven and finish up with a roasting while you do other things.

Pour in an inch of liquid and cover the pan for a sauté, steam, or braise.

BLANCHING

Blanching vegetables is quick and easy, and allows you to add salt or aromatic herbs to the water for some additional flavor. Thomas Keller of The French Laundry likes to blanch vegetables in water that is as salty as the sea. Macrobiotic cooks say that just one grain of quality sea salt in a pot of water is sufficient to draw the minerals and flavor out of the interior of the vegetable. At Tassajara, we follow the middle way—a couple of tablespoons of table salt per gallon of water.

Simply bring a large pot of water to a boil, add salt, and drop in the vegetables. Use the largest pot you can find so that there is a large volume of water to maintain the cooking temperature when the vegetables are added. As soon as the vegetables are done cooking, it is a good idea to put them in a bowl of ice water or run cold water over them in the sink so that they stop cooking immediately. This is called "shocking" them and is useful in preventing vegetables from being overcooked.

If you don't want to go to the bother of shocking the vegetables, just undercook them a little, knowing that the residual heat will finish the cooking. This works but it takes some experience to get it right, and you end up with either crunchy or mushy veggies.

Most blanched vegetables cook for 5 to 7 minutes depending on size, density, and temperature. Potatoes might take as long as 30 minutes. Taste or pierce with a knife to check doneness.

NOTE: *If you are cooking in any quantity, it is best to blanch vegetables in batches. The cooking actually goes faster if you do just a little at a time. Rather than just dumping all your cold vegetables into the water and waiting for the pot to get up to cooking temperature, add only enough vegetables so that the water only drops from the boil briefly if at all.*

When the internal temperature reaches 140 degrees, the cell walls begin to break down. At this stage, a lot of vegetables will squeak a little between your teeth.

If vegetables come up to a boil too slowly, they go from being crisp and firm to flabby and limp.

Near the boiling point (212 degrees F), the cellulose framework breaks down into smaller segments easily separated by the teeth, and the vegetables are perceived as tender.

Boiling for too long can cause the cell walls to disintegrate almost completely, which makes for a smooth purée or a mushy pea.

STEAMING

One of the quickest and healthiest ways to cook vegetables is in a steamer basket (available in most grocery stores). Simply add ¾ inch of water to the bottom of the pot. Put cut veggies in the basket and steam. Kale takes about 7 minutes. Potatoes, beets, and yams need longer, about 15 to 25 minutes. Garnish with butter, or olive oil, or a vinaigrette. Salt and pepper to taste.

PRESSURE COOKING

Pressure cookers used to be scary things. I know many people who have had traumatic experiences with geysers of boiling hot food erupting in their kitchens. The new style of pressure cooker has eliminated most of the danger with double-locking lids and easy-to-follow instructions.

Pressure-cooking is an essential skill in eating whole grains and legumes, especially if you are cooking at any altitude. Pressure-cooking reduces cooking time up to 70 percent. Unsoaked beans only need 45 minutes to 1 hour of fuel to cook instead of hours and hours on a flame over the course of most of a morning or afternoon. Brown rice is done in

30 minutes, and you can cook apples for applesauce in 3 or 4 minutes.

Pressure cookers are great time-saving devices, and they help conserve our dwindling fuel supply. When you use a pressure cooker, you are creating a cooking environment with much higher atmospheric pressure. You can cook food at a temperature of 250 degrees, which is the equivalent of cooking beans or rice in a pit 19,000 feet below sea level! The starches inside the legumes and grains burst and turn into a gelatinized matrix of deliciously digestible carbohydrates and proteins unlike anything else. Pressure cooking is the fastest, most fuel-efficient method of cooking, and many people around the world use them out of necessity.

Pressure cookers are all a little different. Follow the instructions that came with yours and use it often enough so that you get to know the particulars of your burners and flames.

The basic method is to fill the pot up to three-fourths full with water and whatever you are cooking, then bring it to a boil and put the lid on. Turn the heat down to medium-high, seal the lid, and continue cooking until steam starts escaping from the safety valve. Turn heat down to maintain a gentle simmer and enough pressure in the pot to create a steady stream of hissing steam.

If a recipe says to pressure-cook for 20 minutes, it means to start the cooking time when the pressure has built up. You can stop cooking more quickly by putting the pot in the sink and running cold water over it or you can let the pressure come down naturally on its own. Vegetables generally should be brought down quickly but brown rice and beans appreciate the extra time sitting and cooking as the pressure drops naturally.

Vegetable Stock and Variations

Stocks are great to have on hand for making soups and sauces, and as a cooking liquid. Vegetables, grains, and beans cooked in stock have more flavor, and by changing the ingredients in the stock, you can impart or enhance particular flavors in a dish.

2 onions	7 or so parsley stalks
3 carrots	2 bay leaves
4 celery stalks	1 tablespoon crushed black peppercorns
2 garlic heads	8 cups cold water
½ bunch fresh thyme	

Peel the onions and cut them in half. Scrub the carrots and celery and then roughly chop. Cut the garlic heads in half crosswise, so that all the cloves have been cut in half. Place these ingredients, together with the thyme, parsley, bay leaves, and peppercorns into a pot with about 8 cups of water. Bring to a boil and cook at the barest hint of a simmer for 30 minutes. Strain the stock into a fine mesh colander. The stock can be further reduced after it has been strained.

NOTE: *Any clean, fresh vegetable trimmings like leek greens, potato skins, carrot peelings, or mushroom ends can be used in stock. Other possible ingredients are herbs or spices like coriander or fennel seeds, dried mushrooms, lentils, Parmesan cheese rinds, or nutritional yeast. Vegetables can be sautéed or roasted before being added to the stock, if desired.*

VARIATIONS: *Mushroom Stock*

For dishes that feature mushrooms, it's great to add 1 to 2 cups dried shiitakes or porcini mushrooms as well as any trimmings to the above stock recipe. This creates a hearty mushroom stock. The reconstituted mushrooms can be retrieved from the stockpot and used in the final dish.

Thai Vegetable Stock

For Thai dishes and curries, a stock can be made that is infused with traditional Thai herbs and spices. Leave the celery out of the stock above and add one or two thick slices of galangal, 2 stalks of sliced lemon grass, and a handful of kaffir lime leaves.

Simple Garlic Vinaigrette and Variations

This is where art and science come together. The emulsification of oil and vinegar into a thick rich sauce is one of those magical transformations that cooks should never take for granted.

2 garlic cloves	2 tablespoons vinegar
Salt and pepper	⅓ to ½ cup olive oil

In a mortar and pestle, crush the garlic, salt, and pepper for about 2 minutes, or until frothy and fragrant. Pounding the garlic with the salt breaks down the cell walls, releasing more flavor than mincing it with a knife. If you don't have a mortar and pestle, use a garlic press or mince with a knife, crushing the garlic against the cutting board with the side of the knife as you chop it. After the garlic is crushed to a pulp, pour the vinegar over it and let sit for a while. The vinegar actually cooks the garlic and helps round out some of the sharp edges, mellowing the flavor while infusing the vinegar with the essence of garlic. Right before serving your salad, add the olive oil to finish.

NOTE: *Some tricks to getting a nice emulsification for your salad dressing:*

Use a glass jar with a tight-fitting lid. Pour everything in and shake with vigor! After a very short time (usually no more than a minute), you will have a wonderfully well-emulsified dressing.

The classic way is in a bowl with a whisk. Put the vinegar and seasonings in a medium-large bowl and pour in the olive oil in a thin stream while whisking as fast as you can. You are trying to break up the stream of olive oil into a thousand little droplets the moment it hits the surface of the liquid in the bowl. So whisk fast and hard without too much splashing around. After about half the olive oil has been poured in and the dressing seems to be thickening up, you can begin pouring the oil a little more quickly.

MAKES ABOUT ½ CUP

VARIATIONS:

Cumin Lime Vinaigrette

¼ teaspoon toasted and ground cumin	2 tablespoons lime juice
½ teaspoon salt	3 to 4 tablespoons olive oil
Freshly ground black pepper	

MAKES ABOUT ½ CUP

Classic French Vinaigrette

½ to 2 tablespoons good wine vinegar

Salt

½ teaspoon dry mustard

Pinch of dried herbes de Provence

6 tablespoons oil

MAKES ABOUT ½ CUP

Balsamic Vinaigrette

2 garlic cloves, minced

Salt

2 tablespoons balsamic vinegar

6 to 8 tablespoons olive oil

MAKES ABOUT ½ CUP

Dijon Vinaigrette

2 garlic cloves, minced

Salt

1 tablespoon balsamic vinegar

1 tablespoon Dijon mustard

6 to 8 tablespoons olive oil

MAKES ABOUT ½ CUP

Honey Dijon Vinaigrette

½ cup white wine vinegar

1 tablespoon Dijon mustard

1 teaspoon minced garlic

1 tablespoon honey

Pinch of salt and pepper

¾ cup olive oil

MAKES ABOUT 1½ CUPS

North African Vinaigrette

3 teaspoons orange zest

¼ cup fresh blood orange juice or regular
    orange juice

1 teaspoon salt

⅛ teaspoon Turkish pepper or cayenne

½ teaspoon coriander

½ teaspoon cumin

½ teaspoon dry mustard

1 teaspoon honey

½ teaspoon paprika

⅔ cup extra virgin olive oil

MAKES 1 SCANT CUP

Dressings

Sesame Vinegar Dressing

4 teaspoons sesame tahini

2 teaspoons soy sauce

2 teaspoons rice vinegar

2 teaspoons sake or mirin (or substitute
    1 teaspoon honey)

MAKES ABOUT 3 TABLESPOONS

Sesame Miso Dressing

2 tablespoons white sesame seeds

2 tablespoons white miso

2 tablespoons sake or mirin

Toast the sesame seeds in a pan until lightly browned. Cool, then grind in a coffee or spice grinder.
Whisk the ground sesame seeds with the miso and sake.

MAKES ABOUT ⅓ CUP

Basic Ingredients and Sauces

Garlic Oil

This simple infusion of garlic is a quick dipping sauce for bread and vegetables, and is a delicious component in tofu marinades, dressings, and sauces of all kinds at Tassajara.

1 cup olive oil	6 garlic cloves, minced

Heat olive oil and garlic in a small pan over medium-low heat until it begins to smell fragrant. Use immediately or strain out the garlic and store in a cool dark place. Heating the oil makes it more likely to turn rancid, so taste before using; but it should last weeks in the refrigerator.

MAKES 1 CUP

Rosemary Garlic Oil

½ cup olive oil	2 teaspoons chopped rosemary
4 to 6 garlic cloves, minced	

Combine ingredients and heat over medium-low heat until it smells fragrant. Try not to brown the garlic, as that can make it bitter.

MAKES ½ CUP

Reduced Balsamic Vinegar

In a small saucepan over high heat, reduce the vinegar to half its original volume. (For a more intensely flavored reduction, bring the volume down to one-third.) Be careful that all of the vinegar doesn't boil away as you reduce it. Cool and store in a sealed jar along with your other vinegars, or refrigerate. Serve drizzled over fruit or cheese or use to add zip to eggs or to garnish cooked or raw vegetables.

Ghee

Put a pound or two of butter in a heavy-bottom pot over low heat. If you are in a hurry, cut the butter up a bit and start the pot out over high heat for 3 to 5 minutes to get the melting started. Turn heat down to low as soon as there is one-eighth inch of melted butter in the pan.

Do not disturb the butter until the top layer turns brown and begins to fall to the bottom. Carefully pour the clear ghee into a separate container without disturbing the browned milk solids in the bottom of the pot. Ghee is basically clarified butter. Traditionally, ghee is made in large batches in a big iron kettle over a bed of hot coals. Ghee, or clarified butter, is great to cook with because it has a much higher smoking point than regular butter. Clarifying the butter allows you to cook at much higher temperatures without foul flavors forming.

Ghee is something you can start on the stove and then leave alone. You shouldn't even stir it while it's cooking. Let the butter melt slowly and begin to boil and bubble gently enough that the top layer of milk solids can slowly sink to the bottom of the pot. The milk solids will brown, imparting a nuttiness that is distinctive to carefully cooked ghee.

Garam Masala

This is a great spice mix to have on hand. Stored, it lasts a year or so; but, of course, it is never as good as on the day you make it.

1 tablespoon coriander seeds	1 teaspoon cinnamon
½ tablespoon cumin seeds	1 teaspoon tumeric
1 teaspoon fenugreek seeds	½ tablespoon cardamom
6 cloves	Pinch of cayenne

Toast all of the seeds and cloves separately in a small dry skillet over medium-high heat. If the skillet is hot enough, this should be just a matter of 15 to 20 seconds per spice. Heat them just until they release their delicious scent. If they get too brown or burnt-smelling, start over. After each seed is toasted, transfer to a mortar and pestle or spice grinder. If you use an electric coffee grinder, you can grind them all together, but it is nice to grind them separately to begin with so that the harder seeds like fenugreek can get as finely ground as the softer spices. Once all the seeds and cloves are ground, simply stir together with the remaining spices.

Coconut Milk

Canned coconut milk is readily available, but it is nice to know how to make it from shredded coconut if you need to. It is much more environmentally friendly to ship dried coconut halfway around the world than a bunch of canned liquid.

About 1 cup water

8 ounces shredded unsweetened dried coconut

Bring water to a boil in a small saucepan and add coconut. Water should barely cover the coconut, so add more water if needed. Cook over low heat for 2 to 3 minutes, turn off the heat, and cover; let stand 10 minutes. Pour through two layers of cheesecloth and then squeeze the coconut in the cheesecloth until it is dry.

NOTE: *Turning a whole coconut into shredded coconut is fairly straightforward if not easy. Pierce two of the three soft spots at the end of the coconut with an ice pick, awl, or screwdriver. Drain the water out of the coconut and reserve for some other use. Put the whole drained coconut in a preheated 350-degree oven until it cracks, about 20 to 30 minutes. Split the coconut open with a hammer. Separate the coconut shell from the coconut meat using a sharp knife. Put the meat in a food processor and pulse until shredded.*

MAKES ABOUT 2 CUPS

Gomashio

For some, this salty condiment is a real treat; for others, it is more of an acquired taste.

1 cup sesame seeds   1 tablespoon sea salt

Toast sesame seeds in a dry skillet over medium-high heat. When they begin to pop and release their fragrances, grind with salt and serve. For large quantities, mix the seeds and salt, and then toast in a thin layer on sheet pans in a 350-degree oven.

NOTE: *Gomashio is any ratio of toasted sesame seeds and good sea salt ground up together in a suribachi—a ceramic bowl with grooves in the bottom that works like a mortar and pestle. At Tassajara, we have an old-fashioned hand-cranked grain mill that cracks the sesame seeds very nicely but requires most of an afternoon. A few seconds in a food processor or coffee grinder also works pretty well.*

At Tassajara, we used the ratio of about 14 parts brown sesame seeds to 1 part salt, but recipes say anywhere from 8 to 20 parts sesame seeds to 1 part salt. Jars of gomashio sold commercially can be good if there is a high turnover at your store. They are generally pretty salty and can be extended with other sesame seeds from the bulk section. Make sure to check the label to make sure that there is no MSG or "flavor" listed in the ingredients. Gomashio should be nothing more than sesame seeds and salt.

Harissa

This simple seasoning paste can be used in all sorts of applications. You can add it to soup or use it as a nice base for a tofu marinade. Many recipes use only dried hot chile peppers, which make for a very spicy condiment. Use a blend of red bell peppers and hot peppers so that you can use more of the hot peppers without causing too many tears. Harissa keeps well refrigerated. Pour a thin layer of olive oil over the top to keep it from drying out or discoloring.

2 red bell peppers, roasted and peeled
8 dried ancho or guajillo chiles
4 garlic cloves
1½ teaspoons toasted and ground
   cumin seeds

1½ teaspoons toasted and ground
   coriander seeds
1 teaspoon ground caraway seeds
Salt

Preparing the peppers is the most time-consuming part of this rather quick recipe. If you have a gas burner, roast red bell peppers right over the flame, turning regularly with a pair of tongs. If you don't have a gas burner, cut the peppers in half through the stem and remove the stem and seeds. Oil the skin and put the peppers cut-side-down on a baking sheet. Press them down to flatten a bit. Broil the peppers for a few minutes or bake at 400 degrees for about 10 to 15 minutes. Cook until most of the skin is blistered and parts of it are beginning to blacken. Put the peppers to rest in a covered bowl to steam for about 10 to 15 minutes. The skins should be easy to peel off.

The dried chiles should be wiped off and toasted briefly over a flame or in the oven. Just a few seconds per side if you are toasting them on the stovetop. If you broil or bake them in the oven, it should be no more than a few minutes before they begin to smell fragrant and toasty. Don't let them start smoking or they will be bitter. Soak in hot water until softened, about 15 minutes.

Blend the peppers and garlic with the cumin, coriander, caraway, and salt. A food processor works well, but traditionally harissa would be ground by hand in a mortar and pestle.

MAKES ABOUT 1 CUP

Roasted Red Pepper Romesco Sauce

This sauce works great as a condiment for grilled or roasted vegetables such as zucchini, eggplant, carrots, onions, and cauliflower.

4 red bell peppers, seeded and quartered
4 garlic cloves, peeled
Olive oil, as needed
1 cup almonds

2 tablespoons red wine vinegar
1½ teaspoons salt
2 tablespoons paprika
1 teaspoon crushed red pepper flakes

Preheat oven to 350 degrees. Brush peppers and garlic lightly with olive oil and bake until soft, about 20 minutes. Meanwhile, roast the almonds on a baking sheet until slightly browned and fragrant, about 8 to 9 minutes. Place roasted peppers, garlic, almonds, vinegar, salt, and spices in a food processor and process until smooth. Slowly stream in the 1 cup olive oil while the processor is running.

MAKES 2–3 CUPS

Simple Tomato Sauce

A few hours at most is all a sauce needs to simmer and come together. Use good-quality organic tomatoes for this tasty recipe.

1 to 2 cups chopped onions
Olive oil
2 to 4 tablespoons minced garlic
1 to 2 tablespoons dried herbs such as
    rosemary, thyme, and oregano

½ to 1 cup red wine (optional)
1 (14-ounce) can tomatoes with liquid
Salt and pepper
Sugar (optional)

Cook onions in olive oil over high heat until soft and brown. A traditional bolognese sauce is rich with fat from ground meat. Don't be afraid to add lots of olive oil for richness. Add garlic and herbs to the onion and let this brown; deglaze the pan with red wine, scraping up all the yummy bits. Add tomatoes and simmer for at least 15 minutes. Finish with salt and freshly ground pepper. Sometimes a pinch or more of sugar can bring out subtle flavors in the sauce while tempering the acidity of the tomatoes.

MAKES ABOUT 3 CUPS

Roasted Tomato Sauce

Tomatoes can get very juicy when you roast them, so make sure that the pan you use has a lip. Don't use flat cookie sheets! This is a really easy sauce for enchiladas or a wonderful base for soup.

3 pounds tomatoes, washed and stemmed
Olive, canola, or corn oil, as needed
2 cups chopped onions
2 teaspoons cumin

4 garlic cloves, minced
2 jalapeños, washed and minced (or substitute a few canned chipotle peppers)
Water or stock

Preheat the oven to 500 degrees. Coat the tomatoes with oil and then spread out on a couple of sheet pans. Roast the tomatoes for 10 or 12 minutes. They should begin to blacken in spots and release some of their juices. Flip over part way through cooking if they aren't cooking evenly. Let the tomatoes cool enough so that you can comfortably remove the peels. Don't discard the juice!

While the tomatoes cook, sauté the onions in a little oil over high heat until they begin to brown. Add the cumin and garlic, and cook for 3 or 4 minutes more.

In a food processor or blender, purée the tomatoes, onions, and peppers into a sauce. Add a little water or stock if you like.

MAKES 4 CUPS

Taste and See

—EVERETT WILSON

My tenzo's instructions were always pretty straightforward.

"Here is the recipe," he'd say, handing me a 4 x 6-inch index card. "Don't follow it. Start by sautéing some onions, and when it is time to add some herbs, come find me and we'll taste and see."

After some time, I learned to taste and see for myself.

Creamy Saffron Tomato Sauce

This quick sauce is a nice complement to polenta, crêpes, potatoes, pasta, and vegetables of all sorts.

2 tablespoons olive oil
1 cup chopped onions
1 teaspoon salt
½ teaspoon ground cardamom
½ teaspoon ground cinnamon
1 (14-ounce) can diced tomatoes, or 1
  pound chopped fresh tomatoes

1 pinch saffron threads
1 (14-ounce) can coconut milk, or about
  2 cups homemade
1 to 2 teaspoons sugar (optional)
Salt and freshly ground black pepper

Heat a heavy-bottom saucepan over medium-high heat. Add olive oil. When oil is hot, sauté onions with salt until soft and translucent, about 7 to 10 minutes. Add the spices and tomatoes, and heat to a simmer. Add saffron and coconut milk, and heat through. Season with sugar, salt, and pepper. Purée with a stick blender or food processor.

MAKES ABOUT 4 CUPS

Fresh Basil Pesto

The texture and aroma of this pesto is quite different if you take the time to pound it by hand in a mortar and pestle. All of the volatile oils and flavor components get released when the cells get pounded rather than neatly cut by the blade of a food processor.

1 bunch (about 1½ cups) basil leaves
2 garlic cloves
¼ cup pine nuts

½ to ¾ cup grated Parmesan cheese
½ to ¾ cup olive oil
Salt and pepper

If you make this by hand, pound the basil leaves in a mortar and pestle. Start with a few at a time and work the rest in gradually. Add the garlic cloves and continue pounding until garlic is completely mashed. Add the pine nuts and continue pounding into a thick paste. Add the Parmesan cheese and continue to mix and pound. When this is all mixed in, slowly add the olive oil until it is the desired texture. Season with salt and pepper, and serve or store in glass containers with a thin layer of oil coating the top of the pesto. Pesto can be refrigerated for about a week or frozen for up to a year.

MAKES ABOUT ½ CUP

Béchamel Sauce

Béchamel is one of the classic roux-based sauces that Julia Child says "are the old standbys of home cooking . . . you will use them countless times in one guise or another." It can be flavored with herbs and spices, or mixed with some grated cheese for a cheese sauce. To make a nice cheese sauce, stir in about ¼ cup grated cheese per cup of béchamel. Let the sauce cool for a few minutes before stirring in the cheese, or you run the risk of having a very stringy sauce.

4 cups milk	6 to 7 tablespoons flour
5 tablespoons butter	1 teaspoon salt

Heat the milk in a small saucepan. It does not have to boil but needs to be hot enough not to shock the roux you make in the next step.

In a heavy-bottom saucepan, melt the butter. Add the flour and mix it into a paste. Let this roux bubble and cook until it is just beginning to color. Remove from the heat, pour in all but three-fourths of the hot milk, and whisk vigorously. When it is blended together, return to a fairly high heat and stir slowly with a wooden spoon that reaches the corners of your pan. Keep the sauce from sticking while it simmers for 2 to 3 minutes. If you don't bring up the heat and really cook the sauce for a few minutes, the starches in the sauce can remain sort of pasty and uncooked. Add the remaining milk a little at a time until the consistency is how you like it. The sauce should thicken up so that if you run your finger over the back of your wooden spoon, there should be a trail left behind.

MAKES ABOUT 4 CUPS SAUCE

Black Bean Sauce

This sauce adds a very authentic Chinese flavor to any vegetable. Simply make the sauce and stir-fry vegetables right in the wok with the sauce. It also makes a nice marinade for tofu.

2 tablespoons fermented black beans
2 to 4 tablespoons dry sherry or Shaoxing
1 to 2 tablespoons sesame or peanut oil
1 tablespoon garlic purée

1 tablespoon minced ginger
1 teaspoon sugar
1 tablespoon soy sauce

Combine the beans and sherry. Lightly crush the beans, but be careful not to turn them into a paste. You want some little nuggets of flavor. Let stand for at least 10 minutes.

In a wok or skillet, heat oil over medium-high heat, add beans, garlic, ginger, and sugar, and stir to combine. Bring to a simmer and cook until the mixture begins to reduce. Add soy sauce and simmer 2 minutes more.

NOTE: *Fermented black beans are a salted, preserved flavoring component in Chinese cooking. The brand we use at Tassajara is Yang Jiang Preserved Beans. They come in a cardboard container with a yellow and brown label. Fermented beans are preserved, so they last indefinitely in a cool, dry, dark cupboard or the refrigerator. Always rinse fermented black beans in cool water before using to wash away a little bit of the monosodium glutamate and the excess salt. For an authentic seasoning component in any stir-fry, simply crush them and mix with a wooden spoon. Then mix with a little soy sauce, garlic, and ginger, and start cooking.*

SERVES 4–6

Easy Red Mole (page 216)

Mole

—CRISTINA CRUZ

Roasted poblano peppers and dark chocolate mole was on the dinner menu for the seventy guests five hours later. I started roasting peppers on an open flame while the other cook was mixing ingredients for dessert. The beans were simmering to tenderness in the big pot. I stirred them. The many steps for the mole made it look more delicious: peel after roasting, blend, add to broth made the night before, simmer for how many hours? The final touch was to add the dark chocolate "to taste." So I did. Once the beans were cooked I laid them to rest in four covered, deep stainless steel pans and set the mole in identical pans, all stacked in two neat piles on top of the stove, awaiting serve-up time.

The clock showed one and a half hours before serve-up. We were on time. Then, a loud domino clash of metal filled the kitchen. I turned around to watch a tsunami of beans and mole creeping towards me. Pans and lids were scattered everywhere. The other cook stood petrified by the stove. Her eyes screaming a silent guilty terror. Although my eyes were gazing at the sea of despair; my mind was at peace. I was not angry, sad, and definitely not happy either. For just one moment there were no guests, no kitchen, no clock ticking, and no chaos—just beans, mole, and me, separate but still blended as one. For just that one moment, all was well.

After dinner and late that evening, towers of opened 64-ounce cans, with labels reading pinto beans and tomato sauce, were overflowing the recycle container; beans and mole weighed down the compost buckets. The other cook and I never spoke about the casualty. She did not apologize, and I did not expect her to do so. The next day we enjoyed our day off, hiking along the creek and feeling at peace.

Easy Red Mole

This rich mole is delicious over enchiladas or layered in a casserole of leftover beans underneath corn bread, and it works well with tofu and vegetables. It is much simpler than a lot of traditional moles, and you can always depend on having most of these ingredients in the pantry or fridge. Mole comes from the Aztec word for "sauce." Every region in Mexico has its own unique version of a chile paste thickened with ground seeds or corn. Traditionally, moles are served almost exclusively for special occasions.

3 cups chopped white onions
Oil
½ to 1 teaspoon toasted and ground cumin
    seeds, or use powdered
½ teaspoon toasted and ground coriander
    seeds, or use powdered
¾ teaspoon oregano (substitute some
    epazote for some of this if you have it)
2 to 3 teaspoons minced garlic
3 to 4 dried ancho chile peppers, toasted,
    seeded, and stemmed

½ to 1 tablespoon canned chipotle peppers
    in adobo sauce
½ teaspoon cinnamon
¼ teaspoon powdered cloves
1½ cups toasted almonds or pecans
½ cup raisins
2 tomatoes or 1 (14.5-ounce) can, diced
2 tablespoons cocoa powder
Salt and pepper

Sauté onions in oil over high heat until translucent and beginning to brown, about 20 minutes. Add cumin, coriander, and oregano. Turn the heat down, add the garlic, and let this mixture cook while you prepare the chiles, about 20 minutes.

Put the chiles in a metal pan or bowl and cover them with boiling water. They should float quite freely. When the chiles are softened and plump, drain the water. It is tempting to save the water, but it is always really bitter even if it smells good. If the skins come off of the chiles easily, remove them. The chiles are now ready to be blended into a paste.

Blend the toasted anchos with the cooked onions, chipotle peppers, cinnamon, cloves, nuts, raisins, and enough tomatoes to get the blender to work. Process to a fine purée. Add some water or more tomatoes if you want a thinner sauce, or grind with a big pestle until it is a paste.

NOTE: *Traditional cooks fry this paste in hot oil in a skillet. This step adds a certain depth to the sauce that has to be weighed against the chef's willingness to get burned by the volatile splatter. If you do want to fry your sauce, try doing it in a wok or invest in a mesh splatter guard for your skillet.*

Combine the paste with the rest of the tomatoes and bring it to a simmer. Make a slurry with the cocoa and a little liquid and add it to the mole, then add salt and pepper. Use with enchiladas or as a sauce for tofu or vegetables, or add it to a pot of cooked beans to make a delicious chili.

NOTE: *Toast the ancho chile pods over an open flame for a few seconds or spread them out on sheet pans and bake them in a hot oven at 425 degrees just until they begin to get fragrant. They should color a bit but not start smoking and burning. Let the chiles cool. Tear the stems out and remove as many seeds as you like. The more seeds, the more heat. Be careful whenever you handle chiles. The oils are vicious and can burn your hands. Wash well with soapy water after working with chiles, especially before you touch your face. Some folks say that coating your hands in oil will protect them from burning. It seems to work if you have a lot of chiles to process. If you are only working with a couple, it hardly makes sense. Many cooks wear gloves when working with chiles.*

SERVES 6–8

index

Metric Conversion Chart

U.S.	Canadian	Australian	Fahrenheit	Celsius
1/4 teaspoon	1 mL	1 ml	250	120
1/2 teaspoon	2 mL	2 ml	275	140
1 teaspoon	5 mL	5 ml	300	150
1 tablespoon	15 mL	20 ml	325	160
1/4 cup	50 mL	60 ml	350	180
1/3 cup	75 mL	80 ml	375	190
1/2 cup	125 mL	125 ml	400	200
2/3 cup	150 mL	170 ml	425	220
3/4 cup	175 mL	190 ml	450	230
1 cup	250 mL	250 ml	475	240
1 quart	1 liter	1 litre	500	260

Liquid and Dry Measures | Temperature Conversion Chart

when all the dishes are done . . .

THE TASSAJARA BATH

five courses, cooked and plated.
deep belly breaths
short prayers to the oven gods.
every single 5-gallon pot washed and put away.

you are done.

body sore and belly full, you leave the kitchen
and stumble down the path in the late dusk light
to the baths—oh the bathhouse,
one of three hearts of a Zen temple—
kitchen, meditation hall, bathhouse.

mind still racing from your day of cooking
and staying with your breath,
and your body and mind,
and universe of rice and beans and spices
and tempers lost and found in the Tassajara kitchen,
you shower off the grease and grime of your day
and sink into the clear hot water.

every single muscle and fiber of your being rejoices
floating in the sacred Tassajara spring—
in the lantern light, steam rising, crickets singing.
you feel the bliss of heat and water.
hard work and the tender pain of a heart beginning to open.